METHUEN'S MONOGRAPHS

ON PHYSICAL SUBJECTS

====

General Editor: B. L. WORSNOP, B.SC., PH.D.

AN INTRODUCTION TO
ELECTRONIC ANALOGUE COMPUTERS

An Introduction to
Electronic Analogue Computers

===

by M. G. Hartley, M.Sc. Tech.

Electrical Engineering Department
Faculty of Technology
Manchester University

LONDON: METHUEN & CO LTD
NEW YORK: JOHN WILEY & SONS INC

First published in 1962
© *1962 by M. G. Hartley*
Printed in Great Britain by
Spottiswoode Ballantyne & Co Ltd
London and Colchester
Catalogue No. (Methuen) 2/4316/11

ONULP

Contents

ERRATA:

The appropriate correct forms are given below:

Page 22,   Eqn. 3.9: $\dfrac{G-G'}{G} = \dfrac{1}{M}(1+G)$

Page 53,   Eqn. 4.3(a): $\ddot{\theta}_o + 2\zeta\omega_o\dot{\theta}_o + \omega_o^2\theta_o = \omega_o^2\theta_i$

Page 54,   Eqn. 4.3(b): $\ddot{\theta}_o = \omega_o^2\theta_i - 2\zeta\omega_o\dot{\theta}_o - \omega_o^2\theta_o$

        Eqn. for period T: $T = \dfrac{2\pi}{\omega_o}$

Page 65,   Eqn. 5.1(a): $\mu = \left(\dfrac{-dV_a}{dV_g}\right)_{I_v \text{ const.}}$

Page 76: Preliminary form of eqn. 5.5, $e_3 a_3$ omitted on right hand side of equation

Page 96: Fig. 6.2(a) relates to a *p–n–p* junction transistor

Page 103: Eqn. of p. 103 should read $-I_{co}$ on left hand side

Page 119: Fig. 6.11: numerator of vertical scale is $\theta°C$

Page 128: Three lines from bottom, $-v_1$ volts not v_1 volts
    Omit caption "subtracting element" on Fig. 7.1

Page 144: Fig. 7.13(a) and 7.13(b), omit headings "Thousands, Hundreds, Tens and Units" in each case

Preface

This monograph is aimed at the graduate engineer or scientist who finds a need to know something of analogue computing as an aid to his work but is discouraged when he consults the larger books on the subject.

The level is such that a graduate in Physics or Electrical Engineering ought to be able to read the book comparatively easily. A graduate in other branches of engineering such as Chemical or Mechanical Engineering should be able to understand the basic principles fairly readily. He might have difficulty with some of the sections of less importance to one who is interested in the subject principally as a user of computing equipment.

The book should also prove of value to students in the final year of an Engineering Degree Course for whom short courses in analogue computing are sometimes provided.

Chapter 1 is devoted to a brief historical background. Chapter 2 discusses the whole field of engineering calculation with special reference to analogue and digital techniques. The merits of each are considered. The remainder of the book is devoted to analogue computing alone.

Transfer functions and the like are specified for the most part in the notation of the Laplace Transformation. This has become standard practice in recent years. Its use is briefly explained for those who are accustomed to the D operator methods.

I am indebted to my former colleagues of Ferranti Ltd., Wythenshawe, Manchester, who introduced me to the subject of analogue computing. Thanks are especially due to Dr C. M. Cundall and Mr K. J. Saggerson for their advice and help, and to Mrs J. M. Pring who prepared the manuscript.

M. G. HARTLEY

Faculty of Technology
Manchester University
1962

Historical Background

1.1 Introduction

Aids to calculation have been used from remote times. The abacus is one such. Since the seventeenth century the use of such devices has become increasingly widespread. The primitive desk calculator was introduced by Pascal in 1642, and the slide rule appeared at about the same time. Since then calculating equipment has developed along two distinct lines. One is digital computation, the other is analogue computation.

1.2 Work of Charles Babbage

Early digital computation is typified by the work of Charles Babbage (1792–1871) (Ref. 1.1) who designed and partially built two very ambitious calculating machines. The first – the Difference Engine – was capable of addition. This was performed mechanically using toothed wheels. The intention was to use the machine to calculate functions, and build up mathematical tables using the difference properties of the functions concerned. A table of differences for the evaluation of x^2 is shown in Fig. 1.1. It will be noticed that the second difference has in each case a constant value of 2. Addition of the differences in the appropriate way provides the values of x^2. This is the only arithmetic process involved. Provided that no mechanical failures occur, the accuracy of the solution is dependent on the number of significant figures to which the machine is designed to work. For the section of the table under consideration, a machine working to three significant figures would give precisely the correct solution.

A small working model of the Difference Engine was first demonstrated in 1822. This encouraged Babbage to continue with a larger machine working to twenty decimal places and sixth-order differences. The project was a very ambitious one and was abandoned in 1842 when government support for the venture was withdrawn.

Babbage's second machine was the forerunner of the modern digital

1

computer. The design of the Analytical Engine, as it was called, was begun in 1833, but the project, like that of the Difference Engine, was beyond the resources of the age.

The work of Babbage was forgotten for a century. The principles which he had enunciated were rediscovered by the pioneer workers in

FIG. 1.1. Section taken from a difference table for the evaluation of x^2

x	x^2	First difference	Second difference
8·00	64		
		17	
9·00	81		2
		19	
10·00	100		2
		21	
11·00	121		2
		23	
12·00	144		2
		25	
13·00	169		2

the field of electronic digital computers in the 1940's when the first machines were built in the U.S.A. and the U.K. (Ref. 1.2).

1.3 Work of Kelvin

The alternative analogue approach to the solution of problems is seen when the work of Lord Kelvin (W. Thomson) is considered. In two papers to the Royal Society in 1876, (Ref. 1.3 and 1.4) he showed how mechanical integrators and adders could be interconnected so as to solve continuously a second-order differential equation. One form of mechanical integrator had been invented a year before by his brother J. Thomson (Ref. 1.5).

Two types of mechanical integrator are shown in Fig. 1.2. The disc and wheel type is shown at (a). The independent variable is the rotation of the shaft. The distance of the friction wheel from the axis of the shaft is adjustable. For a small rotation of the shaft, δx radians, there is a corresponding small rotation, δy radians, of the wheel. The relation between them is given by

$$\delta y = k_1 r . \delta x \qquad 1.1$$

where r is the distance of the friction wheel from the axis of the shaft

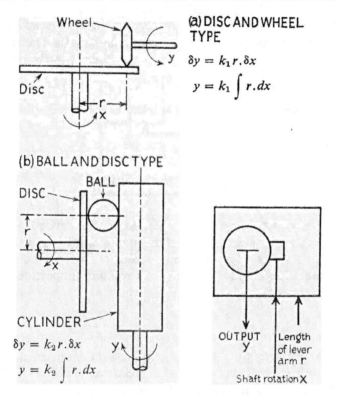

(a) DISC AND WHEEL TYPE

$$\delta y = k_1 r . \delta x$$

$$y = k_1 \int r . dx$$

(b) BALL AND DISC TYPE

$$\delta y = k_2 r . \delta x$$

$$y = k_2 \int r . dx$$

OUTPUT y | Length of lever arm r

Shaft rotation X

(c) SCHEMATIC OF MECHANICAL INTEGRATOR

$$y = k \int r . dx$$

FIG. 1.2. Mechanical Integrators

and k_1 is a constant. The total rotation of the wheel is a measure of the integral of r with respect to x. The total angle y radians, through which the wheel has turned, is taken as the output.

$$y = k_1 \int r.dx \qquad\qquad 1.2$$

At (b) an alternative form of integrator is shown. This is the ball and disc integrator of Thomson. The ball is restrained from tangential motion, but can move radially by an amount proportional to the quantity to be integrated. The rotation of the disc is taken as the independent variable. For a small rotation, δx radians, of the disc, there is a small rotation, δy radians, of the cylinder. As before

$$\delta y = k_2 r.\delta x \qquad\qquad 1.3$$

The total rotation of the cylinder is taken as the output.

$$y = k_2 \int r.dx \qquad\qquad 1.4$$

Unfortunately neither type of integrator can drive an appreciable load without slipping.

Various types of mechanical adder have been devised (Ref. 1.6). These frequently take the form of differential gearboxes using either bevel or spur gears. The two inputs consist of shaft rotations S_1 and S_2 radians. The output is a third shaft rotation proportional to the sum of S_1 and S_2.

1.4 Mechanical differential analysers

No machines using the above principles were constructed until, in 1931, Bush at M.I.T. built the first of a class of machines which have become known as mechanical differential analysers (Ref. 1.7).

Each unit of a mechanical differential analyser carries out one operation, integration or addition, for example. Inputs are shaft rotations, with the angles turned through representing to some convenient scale the variables of the problem. The interconnections between the units are made in such a way that the relations of the various shafts form a translation into mechanical terms of the equation to be solved. Then the rotation of one shaft, representing the independent variable, drives the remainder of the shafts in accordance with the equation represented by the interconnection.

Figure 1.3 shows a schematic arrangement for the solution of the second-order differential equation.

$$\frac{d^2y}{dt^2} + y = 0 \qquad\qquad 1.5$$

which represents a simple harmonic motion.

As with all machines intended for the solution of differential

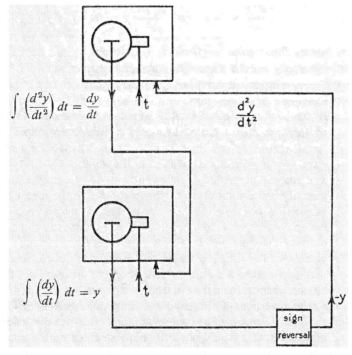

FIG. 1.3. Schematic of Interconnection of Integrators and Sign Reversal unit to solve

$$\frac{d^2y}{dt^2} = -y \quad \text{or} \quad \frac{d^2y}{dt^2} + y = 0$$

equations, the highest derivative is considered first, and is assumed to be available as a shaft rotation which can be applied as the quantity d^2y/dt^2 considered as applied to the first integrator of the machine. The independent variable in this case is time t and is represented by the rotation of both integrator shafts at a steady rate. On integration d^2y/dt^2 yields dy/dt which is applied to the second integrator whose output is y. This quantity then passes through a sign-reversing unit to give $-y$ and is used as the input to the first integrator. The closure of the loop in this way is the essential feature of the differential analyser. In this case such a connection constrains the machine to solve continuously the equation

$$\frac{d^2y}{dt^2} = -y \quad \text{or} \quad \frac{d^2y}{dt^2} + y = 0 \qquad\qquad 1.6$$

In this simple illustration coefficients and initial values have been omitted. The solution for y as a function of time may be taken from the machine in various ways. One convenient manner might be as a graph drawn on a drum revolving at a constant rate.

The principle of closed-loop operation had occurred first to Lord Kelvin when he was endeavouring to solve a second-order differential equation. Initially he considered the solution of a second-order system by the use of two integrators arranged in series, open-loop. The output resulting from an arbitrary function applied to the input of the first integrator is noted. It is then fed to the input of the first integrator. The process is repeated till input and output are equal. This common quantity is the solution to the problem. Kelvin then realized that a connection between the two integrators to provide a closed-loop system would result in a continuous and automatic solution to the differential equation. In the words of Kelvin himself: 'Compel agreement between the function fed into the double machine and that given out by it'. This idea is the basis of the mechanical differential analyser and also the electronic machines.

The precision of the solution using the mechanical differential analyser is dependent on a variety of factors. Slip at the friction wheel of an integrator would naturally have an effect on the accuracy. So also would the quality of the gears and bearings. The mechanical nature of the device would impose serious limitations on the speed of operation. Nevertheless machines of this type are capable of precise work. For example even a small prototype machine constructed largely of standard Meccano parts by Hartree and Porter at Manchester University had an accuracy of the order of 2 per cent (Ref. 1.8).

A variety of mechanical differential analysers are discussed at length in a book by Hartree (Ref. 1.9) and by Crank (Ref. 1.10).

As will be seen in later chapters mechanical differential analysers have been superseded almost entirely by electronic machines. The principle of operation of the electronic machine, however, is very similar to the mechanical one. Even today the mechanical analyser is occasionally used. A large machine of this type has recently been completed in the U.S.S.R. (Ref. 1.11).

REFERENCES

1.1. BOWDEN, B. V. *Faster than Thought*, Pitman, London, 1953.

1.2. WILKES, M. V. *Automatic Digital Computers*, Methuen, London, 1957.

1.3. THOMSON, W. (LORD KELVIN). *Proc. roy. Soc.*, 24, 269, 1876.

1.4. THOMSON, W. (LORD KELVIN). *Proc. roy. Soc.*, 24, 271, 1876.

1.5. THOMSON, J. *Proc. roy. Soc.*, 24, 262, 1876.

1.6. SVOBODA, A. *Computing Mechanisms and Linkages*, Radiation Lab. Series, McGraw-Hill, New York, 1948.

1.7. BUSH, V. *J. Franklin Inst.*, 212, 447, 1931.

1.8. HARTREE, D. R., and PORTER, A. *Mem. Manchr. lit. phil. Soc.*, 79, 51, 1935.

1.9. HARTREE, D. R. *Calculating Instruments and Machines*, Cambridge University Press, 1950.

1.10. CRANK, J. *The Differential Analyser*, Longmans, London, 1947.

1.11. LOSKUTOV. *Priborostroenie*, Sept. 1959. p. 1, and 'Soviet Technology' (review article), *Manchester Guardian*, 15 Dec. 1959.

CHAPTER 2

Comparison of Analogue and Digital Computers

2.1 Introduction

Recent advances in pure and applied sciences have been especially rapid. Progress has only been possible because the advances have occurred at the same time as a tremendous improvement in the facilities for the solution of complex problems. In some cases the

FIG. 2.1. General Engineering calculations

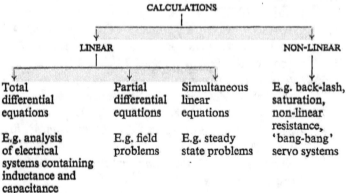

use of computing equipment has merely reduced the time and effort required for the solution of problems. In other cases the use of such equipment has proved essential.

Figure 2.1 shows in schematic form the range of engineering calculations normally encountered. These comprise the two main categories of linear and non-linear. The linear type are sub-divided into total or partial differential equations and simultaneous linear equations. Non-linear problems are typified by such engineering phenomena as back-lash in mechanical systems, saturation in magnetic circuits, and non-linear resistances. Some of the methods for the solution of engineering problems are given in the chart of Fig. 2.2. It will be seen that there are two principal techniques.

FIG. 2.2. Methods for solution of problems

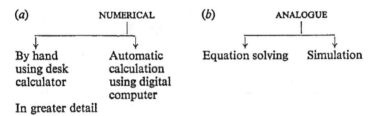

In greater detail

I. Linear equations

1. *Total differential equations*

(a) Numerical

    (i) Finite difference
    (ii) Matrix methods

(b) Analogue

    Equation solving
        (i) Mechanical differential analyser
        (ii) Electronic differential analyser
    Simulation
        Analogue computer used as a simulator

2. *Partial differential equations*

(a) Numerical

    (i) Relaxation methods
    (ii) Finite difference
    (iii) Matrix methods

(b) Analogue

    Equation solving
        (i) Differential analyser for small departures
        (ii) Electrolytic tank studies
        (iii) Conducting sheets
        (iv) Membrane methods
    Simulation
        Photo-elastic techniques

3. *Simultaneous linear equations*

(*a*) *Numerical*	(*b*) *Analogue*
	Equation solving
(i) Elimination	Transformer analogue
(ii) Trigonometrical	(e.g. Blackburn analyser)
(iii) Relaxation	*Simulation*
	Network analyser

II. Non-linear equations

(*a*) *Numerical*	(*b*) *Analogue*
	Equation solving
Numerical techniques	Differential analyser with
applied over limited	non-linear units or function
ranges of values	generators
assumed to be linear	*Simulation*
	Analogue computers used with
	non-linear units, function
	generators or non-linear
	elements of the system under
	consideration

One is the solution of problems using numerical techniques. A machine used in this work is the modern desk calculator. Basically this is capable of the arithmetic processes of addition, subtraction, multiplication and division. In order to employ it successfully for a complicated problem, the evaluation of a trigonometrical function say, the problem must be expressed in such a fashion as to be capable of solution using simple arithmetic processes. In the example under consideration the function might be written as a suitable power series, which would in turn be evaluated by performing multiplications and additions. For a larger problem, the analysis of the stresses in a stiff frame, for example, an automatic digital computer would probably be used. Once again the problem would have to be presented to the calculating machine in a suitable form. The calculations would be reduced to the simplest arithmetic processes. The operator of the desk machine with his knowledge of the various stages of the calculation would be replaced by the computer programme providing the detailed instructions for each section of the calculation. Some form of storage, magnetic drum, cathode-ray tube, mercury tank, or punched tape, would take the place of the operator's notebook used to record intermediate results when the desk machine was in use.

An alternative approach to the solution of engineering problems is the use of analogue computing equipment. For the solution of differential equations as such, some form of differential analyser is normally used. When the emphasis is on the physical quantities themselves, the same machine may be used as an analogue computer or simulator. The distinction between these two functions of analogue computing equipment is important and is discussed at length later in this section.

If partial differential equations are considered for small departures a differential analyser again may be used. The other methods used for the solution of partial differential equations are most interesting and often highly ingenious. In some, such as the electrolytic tank method, (Ref. 2.1), a system conforming to the same field equations as the problem under consideration is used as an indirect model. The solutions obtained are then applied to the original situation. Conducting sheets (Ref. 2.2), membrane methods with rubber sheets (Ref. 2.3) or soap bubbles (Ref. 2.4) are used in a similar way. Photo-elastic methods (Ref. 2.5) are used as more direct analogues for stress analysis in mechanical and civil engineering. Here transparent models are stressed in a similar manner to the structure under consideration. Provided that material used is suitable, lines of equal stress are observed in the model when it is illuminated by polarized light. The method is applicable to both two- and three-dimensional problems. Unfortunately a detailed consideration of the above methods for the solution of partial differential equations falls outside the scope of this book.

The above general survey of the field of engineering calculations indicates that for the most part computing equipment falls into one or other of the broad categories of digital or analogue. For a full treatment of analogue methods the reader is referred to Ref. 2.6. While it is occasionally difficult to decide the category of a particular machine, the basic difference is comparatively simple. The subject is discussed at some length in Ref. 2.7.

The modern digital computer, hand operated or automatic, like the machines of Babbage, operates upon discrete numbers. For example, in the desk machine, numbers are represented by the position of toothed wheels which can take up only certain definite positions. The accuracy of the solution to a problem is dependent on the number of significant figures to which the machine is designed to work. Ambiguities which may occur, for example in division, are restricted to the least significant digit. In the Difference Engine used to calculate a square, the value obtained would be exact provided the machine was constructed so as to operate to a sufficiently great number of significant figures.

On the other hand, the analogue machine, of which the mechanical differential analyser is an example, operates upon quantities which are capable of continuous variation. These quantities, shaft rotation, electrical voltage, and the like, are the analogues of the physical variables of the problem under consideration. They change in a continuous fashion as do the problem variables. The precision with which the analogue quantities can be made to represent the physical variables is the measure of the accuracy of the analogue machine. Imperfections of the analogue machine will be considered later in some detail. If an analogue machine was used for the generation of a square, the accuracy of the result would be dependent on a number of factors. A mechanical device would suffer from the same sort of limitations as the mechanical differential analyser. An electronic device would be dependent on the precision of its components, reference voltages, drift in computing amplifiers and the like. While an improvement in machine performance would produce a more accurate result, an exact value would never be achieved.

Usually a digital computer is employed only as an equation solving device. The position of the beads of the abacus, the wheels of the desk calculator or which valves are conducting and which non-conducting in an electronic machine, represent numbers used in equations rather than physical quantities.

With the analogue machine two possibilities exist. The variable quantities, such as shaft position, may represent mere numbers as is usual in the digital machine. Frequently however they are considered as the analogues of the physical quantities of the problem. In the second case the operator of the analogue machine comes to appreciate the 'feel' of the problem in a very real manner. The use of analogue machines to simulate the behaviour of actual equipment is a very valuable tool in the hands of the engineer. Some examples of the analogue machine used in its two roles will help to illustrate the possibilities.

2.2 Analogue machines used as equation solvers

(i) *Slide rule*. The slide rule is familiar to all. The slide may be adjusted to any position. There is no provision for setting the slide to discrete positions. The precision with which the slide is adjusted to the desired position, and the care with which the solution is read off, determine the accuracy of the solution. In addition the answer is affected by any inherent errors in the device itself such as irregular or inaccurate engraving of the scales. A slide rule in which the slide was capable of taking up only certain definite positions would become a digital machine. Only certain definite input values would be possible. Ambiguities in the solution would be restricted to a single division.

(ii) *Differential analyser*. As already seen such a machine may be mechanical. It may also be electronic. In either case it is used for the solution of differential equations – principally ordinary linear differential equations. In general the solution for each type of machine is obtained by a process of successive integration in a closed-loop configuration. The operator of such a machine is concerned only to solve the equations provided for solution.

2.3 Analogue machines as simulators

(i) *Simulation of vehicle suspension system*. Suppose the design of a shock absorber for a road vehicle is under consideration. The motion of the piston of the shock absorber in the cylinder may be expressed as a second-order differential equation. One important design consideration is the viscosity of the oil used in the system.

When investigating the behaviour of the system using an electronic analogue machine in the role of a simulator, the effect of varying the viscosity of the oil would be readily observed by adjusting a coefficient potentiometer labelled 'oil viscosity'. A family of curves showing the motion of the piston following the application of a shock load for various values of oil viscosity could be drawn up in a comparatively short time. The machine operator would soon appreciate the feel of the problem and would soon reject certain values of viscosity as quite unsuitable. He would concentrate his attention on more important ranges of values. Once the problem had been set up he would give little thought to the differential equation.

If a digital computer was used for the solution of the problem the machine would print out solutions to the differential equation for values of viscosity previously decided upon. Unless a rather sophisticated programme of instructions had been provided for the machine formal solutions would be performed for all the values of viscosity even though some of these solutions corresponded to highly impractical conditions. The operator would be concerned solely with the solution of the differential equation presented to him.

(ii) *Simulations for aircraft and guided weapon studies.* The cost of aircraft and guided weapon studies is very considerable. Malfunction of even a minor item of equipment may result in catastrophic failure of the test vehicle before useful data can be accumulated. Simulation of performance on the ground using an analogue computer enables much valuable information to be collected. In some cases it may be possible to incorporate in the simulation those sections of the equipment which have already been constructed.

For example the early investigation of the yaw motion of an aircraft under design can be restricted to a consideration of the second-order differential equation which relates rudder angle and angular acceleration in yaw. Later the response of the servo system which operates the rudder can be included in the simulation, as can effects of coupling between roll and yaw motion. Approximate values for the coefficients of the terms in the aerodynamic equations governing the motion would be obtained from wind tunnel tests on a prototype model of the proposed aircraft. An actual prototype servo system for rudder control might next be introduced into the simulation. Appropriate electro-mechanical transducers would be used to couple it to the simulator proper. In this way considerable experience would be gained before flight trials commence. Flight trials, wind tunnel tests, and simulator studies may be used to supplement and cross check each other.

Simulator studies can also be used to indicate how a limited number of flight trials can be exploited to best advantage. This is especially true when expense precludes a large number of trials as is the case with most guided weapons.

Tridac, (Three Dimensional Analogue Computer), one of the first, large-scale electronic analogue computers, intended for aircraft and guided weapon studies, is described in a general way in Ref. 2.8.

(iii) *Simulation of nuclear reactors*. The need for gaining operating experience through the medium of simulator studies is self evident in this case. Reference 2.9 is one of many which gives details of the applications of simulation techniques to nuclear reactor studies.

2.4 General purpose analogue computers

These are the type now in wide use. They may be considered as either equation-solving differential analysers, or as simulators, depending on the problem. Such machines are now almost always electronic in operation. The mechanical computers described briefly in the previous chapter suffered from a variety of disadvantages. Some of these are listed below.

(i) Cost and difficulty of manufacturing the machine parts associated with integrators and adders to a sufficiently high standard of precision.

(ii) The physical size of a mechanical computer compares unfavourably with an electronic machine of the same capacity.

(iii) An electronic machine offers the possibility of simulating more complicated functions than a mechanical device.

(iv) Electronic computers may be operated at a higher rate than mechanical differential analysers.

(v) The modern electronic machine offers greater flexibility in operation than the mechanical computer. Interconnections between computing elements is via wiring rather than mechanical linkages. Frequently interconnection is made using a removable 'patch panel'. The complete arrangement of interconnections for a particular problem may be removed on its completion, and a fresh one substituted. The original problem may be restored to the machine later if required.

2.5 Comparison of the speed of operation of analogue and digital machines

The speed of operation of the digital machine depends on its general design. In the 'serial' machine the computations are performed digit by digit in a single arithmetic unit. In the 'parallel' machine there are sufficient arithmetic units to allow the simultaneous addition of all the digits of a pair of numbers. The speed of computation is not normally related to the rate at which the phenomena of a problem are changing. In a digital machine used to compute tables of trajectories for a ballistic missile, for example, there is no relation between the time of flight and the time taken for solution.

The position is rather different when analogue machines are used for the solution of problems. When used merely as equation solvers, the independent variable in the mechanical differential analysers is frequently proportional to time. As will be seen in the next chapter, the independent variable in the electronic machine is always time. The speed of solution is therefore related to the time taken by the physical variables of the problem to reach their steady state. In many cases it is desirable for the time scale of the simulation, or the solution to the differential equation, to be the same as that of the physical problem. This technique is known as operation in 'real' time. For a simulation in which actual items from the system under consideration are attached to the computer it is essential to operate in real time. In other cases it may be possible to include a scale factor. This is operation where 'machine' time is not the same as real time.

For example the solution representing the response of a second-order system to a unit step function may be obtained from an analogue machine operating in a repetitive fashion at a sufficiently rapid rate for a steady picture of the complete response to appear on an oscilloscope display. Machine time in this case need not correspond to real time. If the same machine were used in a simulation of the response of an aircraft control surface which included servo motors from the real system, then it would be essential for the simulation to take place in real time.

2.6 Conclusion

Chapter 1 gave a brief historical background to the general field of computation. In Chapter 2, after discussing the range of problems which requires solution, the essential differences between analogue and digital techniques were considered. Some applications of the analogue machine were mentioned in a general way. Reasons for the abandonment of the mechanical differential analyser were listed. Time scales were discussed.

The remainder of this book will be devoted to the electronic analogue computer – its mode of operation, scope and auxiliary equipment. Examples of its application to problems in various fields will be considered in detail.

REFERENCES

2.1. ZWORYKIN, V. K., MORTON, G. A., RAMBERG, E. G., HILLIER, J., and VANCE, A. W. *Electron Optics and the Electron Microscope*, pp. 389–396. John Wiley, New York, 1945.

2.2. KAYAN, C. F. *Trans. Amer. Soc. mech. Engrs* 67, 713–718, 1945.

2.3. OLIPHANT, M. L., and MOON, P. B. *Proc. Camb. phil. Soc.*, 25, 461, 1929.

2.4. BATEMAN, H. *Proc. roy. Soc.*, (2) 125, 598–618, 1929.

2.5. FROCHT, M. M. *Photo-elasticity*, Vol. 1, 1941; Vol. 2, 1948. John Wiley, New York; Chapman and Hall, London.

2.6. SOROKA, W. W. *Analogue Methods in Computation and Simulation*, McGraw-Hill, New York, 1954.

2.7. SALZER, J. M. *Proc. nat. Electron. Conf.*, Vol. VIII, 621, 1952.

2.8. GARDNER, G. W. H. *J. Instn mech. Engrs*, 2, No. 1, 5, 1955.

2.9. JOHNSON, S. O., CURLEE, N. J., and REIHING, J. V. *IRE Trans. Nuclear Science*, 1958, 1.

CHAPTER 3

The Role of the Operational Amplifier

3.1 Introduction

The mechanical differential analysers considered in Chapter 1 suffered from various disadvantages which have been briefly enumerated. They have been superseded almost entirely by electronic machines. The principle of operation however remains the same. Solutions are obtained by suitable interconnection, in closed-loop fashion, of integrators, summing units and the like.

The essential element of each of these units is a high gain direct-coupled electronic amplifier. With valve amplifiers the analogue quantity is voltage. In the transistor amplifiers now coming into use, voltage is again used as the analogue quantity. The performance of both valve and transistor amplifiers will be considered in greater detail later. For the moment it will suffice to take the valve amplifier and consider it as a unit which possesses the following properties.

(i) *Ability to handle d.c. voltages* such as might occur after the imposition of an input step function.

(ii) *High gain.* The amplifier is considered as a voltage amplifier. Its voltage gain may well be of the order of 10^6. A sign reversal is included.

(iii) *Bandwidth* sufficient to avoid phase-shift or attenuation of the higher frequency components of input waveform.

(iv) *Negligible grid current* at the first stage of the amplifier. A typical value of the grid current might be 10^{-9} A. A negligible grid current implies a very high input impedance to the amplifier.

(v) *Low drift.* All d.c. amplifiers tend to introduce some drift which results in a non-zero output for zero input. This output is not constant but gradually changes. One of the major design problems associated with d.c. amplifiers is the reduction of drift to an acceptably small value. With most d.c. amplifiers used in computing, provision is made for periodic adjustment to give zero output for zero input. The quality of the amplifier determines the frequency with which adjustment has to be made to restore the amplifier to its original balanced condition.

(vi) *Low output impedance.* This has the result that the output of the amplifier is not affected by the magnitude of the load resistance applied to the output of the amplifier. A cathode-follower output stage (see Chapter 5.2) is frequently used for this purpose.

A block diagram of such an amplifier is shown in Fig. 3.1. In this, and all similar diagrams, voltages are referred to an earth line which

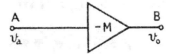

FIG. 3.1. Schematic of high gain d.c. amplifier

is omitted from the diagrams. Let the voltage gain be $-M$. The input is at A, the output is taken at B. For an input voltage v_a, the corresponding output voltage is v_o where

$$v_o = -Mv_a \qquad\qquad 3.1$$

Since the gain is very large the voltage v_a must always be vanishingly small for practical values of v_o. Because the voltage at A tends to zero value, point A is often called a 'virtual earth'.

An amplifier with these properties is often referred to as an 'operational amplifier'. Different combinations of resistance and capacitance at the input to the amplifier, and as feedback elements across the amplifier enable various mathematical operations to be performed.

3.2 Application to sign change

In Fig. 3.2, R_l is a resistor connected to the amplifier input, R_f is a feedback resistor connected across the amplifier between A and B. Since no current flows into the grid of the amplifier input stage

$$i_{in} = i_f \qquad\qquad 3.2$$

where i_{in} is the current flowing in the resistor R_l, and i_f is the current in R_f.

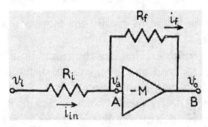

FIG. 3.2. Amplifier used for sign reversal and gain change

Application of Ohm's Law to eqn. 3.2 gives

$$\frac{v_i - v_a}{R_i} = \frac{v_a - v_o}{R_f}$$

or

$$R_f(v_i - v_a) = R_i(v_a - v_o)$$

but

$$v_a = -\frac{v_o}{M} \quad \text{from eqn. 3.1}$$

Hence

$$R_f v_i + R_f \frac{v_o}{M} = -R_i \frac{v_o}{M} - R_i v_o$$

or

$$v_o \left\{ \frac{R_f}{M} + \frac{R_i}{M} + R_i \right\} = -R_f v_i$$

Therefore

$$\frac{v_o}{v_i} = \frac{-R_f M}{R_f + R_i(1+M)} \qquad\qquad 3.3$$

Since M is very large

$$\frac{v_o}{v_i} \simeq -\frac{R_f}{R_i} \qquad\qquad 3.4(a)$$

If M is infinite

$$\frac{v_o}{v_i} = -\frac{R_f}{R_i} \qquad\qquad 3.4(b)$$

Let $R_i = R_f$, when for finite values of M

$$\frac{v_o}{v_i} \simeq -1 \qquad\qquad 3.5$$

Since $v_o \simeq -v_i$, a sign change has been achieved.

3.3 Application to scale change

In many cases it may be desirable to change the magnitude of the analogue quantity in addition to changing its sign. This is multiplication by a constant k

$$v_o = -kv_i \qquad 3.6$$

The analysis is just as for the previous case as far as eqn. 3.4(a). The ratio of resistors R_f/R_i is simply made equal to the constant k. Hence,

$$v_o \simeq -\frac{R_f}{R_i}.v_i = -kv_i \qquad 3.7$$

3.4 Effect of finite value of open-loop gain

The voltage gain, $-M$, of the amplifier before the application of the computing elements is frequently called the 'open-loop gain'. The voltage gain when the computing elements have been connected is known as the 'closed-loop gain'.

It is interesting to relate the accuracy with which a sign or scale change is achieved to the open-loop gain of the operational amplifier.

Let the actual value of closed-loop gain be $-G'$ where

$$-G' = \frac{v_o}{v_i} \qquad 3.8(a)$$

Let the ideal closed-loop gain be $-G$, where from eqn. 3.4(b)

$$\frac{R_f}{R_i} = G \qquad 3.8(b)$$

Rearranging eqn. 3.3 we have

$$\frac{v_o}{v_i} = \frac{-R_fM}{R_f+R_i(1+M)} = \frac{-R_f}{R_i+\frac{1}{M}(R_i+R_f)}$$

Substituting from eqn. 3.8 gives

$$\frac{v_o}{v_i} = -G' = \frac{-G}{\left\{1+\frac{1}{M}(1+G)\right\}}$$

or
$$-G' = -G\left\{1+\frac{1}{M}(1+G)\right\}^{-1}$$

Expansion using the Binomial Theorem yields

$$-G' = -G\left\{1-\frac{1}{M}(1+G)+\left(\frac{1}{M}\overline{1+G}\right)^{2}+\ldots\right\}$$

Since $M \gg G$ and $M \gg 1$, terms other than the first two in the expansion may be neglected.

Hence
$$G' = G\left\{1-\frac{1}{M}(1+G)\right\}$$

The error in the computation is

$$G-G' = \frac{1}{M}(1+G) \qquad\qquad 3.9$$

Percentage errors introduced for various values of M and G are tabulated in Fig. 3.3. As will be seen from the table, the effect of error

FIG. 3.3. Effect of finite gain in sign change and gain change

The figure shows the percentage error for various values of ideal closed-loop gain G, and open-loop gain M.

		Open-loop gain M					
		10^2	10^3	10^4	10^5	10^6	10^7
Closed-loop gain	0·1	1·1	0·11	0·011	0·0011	0·00011	0·000011
	1·0	2·0	0·20	0·02	0·002	0·0002	0·00002
	10	11·0	1·1	0·11	0·011	0·0011	0·00011
	100	—	10·1	1·01	0·101	0·0101	0·00101

due to finite gain, over a wide range of values of G, is small provided
the open-loop gain is made reasonably large.

Under these circumstances the accuracy will be limited by the
precision with which the ratio of the resistances R_f/R_i is set up, and
maintained, at its initial value.

3.5 Summation

In this case the single feedback resistor R_f is inserted as before. Each
input requiring summation is applied via an input resistor. Figure 3.4

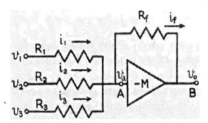

FIG. 3.4 Arrangement for summation

shows an arrangement for the summation of three voltages v_1, v_2,
and v_3, applied to input resistors R_1, R_2, and R_3 respectively.

As in the previous case, grid current is assumed to be zero. The
three input currents i_1, i_2, and i_3 may be equated to the current i_f
through R_f

$$i_1 + i_2 + i_3 = i_f \qquad 3.10$$

substitution gives

$$\frac{v_1 - v_a}{R_1} + \frac{v_2 - v_a}{R_2} + \frac{v_3 - v_a}{R_3} = \frac{v_a - v_o}{R_f} \qquad 3.11$$

now $$v_a = -v_o/M \quad \text{(eqn. 3.1)}$$

Thus rearrangement of eqn. 3.11 gives

$$\frac{v_1}{R_1} + \frac{v_2}{R_2} + \frac{v_3}{R_3} = v_o\left\{-\frac{1}{R_f} - \frac{1}{M}\left(\frac{1}{R_1} + \frac{1}{R_2} + \frac{1}{R_3} + \frac{1}{R_f}\right)\right\}$$

and for large values of M, the last four terms on the right-hand side of the equation may be neglected to give

$$v_o \simeq -R_f\left\{\frac{v_1}{R_1}+\frac{v_2}{R_2}+\frac{v_3}{R_3}\right\}$$

or $$v_o \simeq -\{a_1 v_1 + a_2 v_2 + a_3 v_3\} \qquad 3.12$$

where $$a_1 = \frac{R_f}{R_1}, \quad a_2 = \frac{R_f}{R_2}, \quad \text{and} \quad a_3 = \frac{R_f}{R_3}$$

If $R_1 = R_2 = R_3$

$$v_o \simeq -(v_1 + v_2 + v_3) \qquad 3.13$$

The precision with which this result is achieved depends on the value of the open-loop gain in a similar manner to the previous case. Provided M has a value of the order of 10^5, inaccuracy due to finite gain may be neglected for almost every case. As will be seen from eqn. 3.12, input voltages may be multiplied by constants at the same time as they are assumed. On occasion this may prove a useful facility.

3.6 Integration
For integration a resistor R_i is applied at the input, and a feedback capacitor C is connected across the amplifier. The arrangement is indicated in Fig. 3.5.

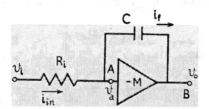

FIG. 3.5. Integration

For a capacitor

$$q = Cv \qquad 3.14(a)$$

where q is the charge on the capacitor, v is the voltage across the plates, and C is the capacitance. The charge q is the time integral of a charging current i, thus

$$q = \int_0^t i.dt \qquad\qquad 3.14(b)$$

Equating 3.14(a) and 3.14 (b) gives

$$\int_0^t i\,dt = Cv$$

On differentiation $\qquad\qquad i = C\,dv/dt \qquad\qquad 3.15$

For zero grid current at the first stage of the operational amplifier

$$i_{\text{in}} = i_f$$

Application of Ohm's Law and substitution from eqn. 3.15 gives

$$\frac{v_i - v_a}{R_l} = C\frac{d}{dt}(v_a - v_o)$$

but $\qquad\qquad v_a = -v_o/M \quad \text{(eqn. 3.1)}$

Hence $\qquad\qquad v_i + \frac{v_o}{M} = -R_l C\frac{d}{dt}\left(v_o + \frac{v_o}{M}\right)$

For large values of M this yields

$$v_i \simeq -R_l C\frac{d}{dt}(v_o)$$

Integrating both sides and rearranging gives

$$v_o \simeq -\frac{1}{R_l C}\int_0^t v_i\,dt + v_{o(t=0)} \qquad\qquad 3.16$$

3

where $v_{o(t=0)}$ is the initial value of output voltage at time $t = 0$. For the moment assume that $v_{o(t=0)}$ has zero value, when,

$$v_o \simeq \frac{1}{R_t C} \int_0^{} v_t dt$$

or
$$v_o \simeq \frac{1}{T} \int_0^t v_t dt \qquad\qquad 3.17$$

where $T = R_t C$ is the time constant of the integrator. This determines the amplitude scaling which is applied. The relation of eqn. 3.17 indicates that a voltage may be integrated with respect to time. Practical limitations and the insertion of initial values will be considered later.

In the electronic analogue computer the independent variable is always time since the integrations are always performed with respect to time. In the mechanical differential analyser the angle turned through by the master crank was the independent variable. If the rotation proceeded at a steady rate, the independent variable could be considered as time, but this was not essential.

In the electronic machine, operation may take place in real time. Alternatively it may be possible to scale the time by some constant value. As was explained in the previous chapter this is not possible if items of physical systems are included in the simulation.

3.7 Integration and summation
Figure 3.6 illustrates summation and integration performed with a single operational amplifier.

$$v_o = -\left\{ \frac{1}{T_1} \int_0^t v_1 \, dt + \frac{1}{T_2} \int_0^t v_2 \, dt \right\} \qquad\qquad 3.18$$

where $T_1 = R_1 C$ and $T_2 = R_2 C$, and initial values have been omitted. If T_1 and T_2 are unequal, v_1 and v_2 may be considered as multiplied by different constants before integration.

In Sections 3.1 to 3.7 no restriction was placed on the form of the input voltage v_i. It may frequently take the form of a step-function or ramp-function. Only in exceptional cases would the input be sinusoidal.

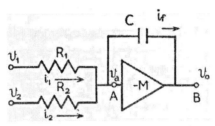

FIG. 3.6. Integration and summation

3.8 The operational amplifier in the general case

So far the operational amplifier has been considered for applications in which resistors have been used at the input, and a resistor or capacitor as a feedback element. Under these conditions there is no restriction on the shape of the input waveform. Consider now what would be the result if impedances other than those mentioned above were inserted as computing elements. Suppose the impedance connected at the amplifier input was Z_i and the feedback element had impedance Z_f.

With sinusoidal operation the current I through a linear circuit of impedance Z is related to the applied voltage V by the relation $Z = \dot{V}/I$. Z may be evaluated by expressing V and I as complex quantities using the well-established methods of the j operator technique. When other than sinusoidal signals are applied more sophisticated methods are required. The Laplace transform technique is very convenient. The reader is referred to one of the textbooks, for example, that given in Ref. 3.1 for a full discussion. What follows here is merely a statement of how the technique may be used in this application.

A voltage v applied to the terminals of a two-terminal network produces a current i given by

$$Z(p)i = \bar{v}$$

where $\bar{\imath}$ and $\bar{v}$ are the Laplace transforms of i and v. A table of some of the more common Laplace transforms is given in Fig. 3.7. $Z(p)$ is called the generalized impedance of the network. The value of $Z(p)$ for a network can be obtained by combining the generalized impedances of the elements which comprise it according to the ordinary

FIG. 3.7. Table of common Laplace transforms

$y(t)$ ($for\ y(t) \geqslant 0$)	$\bar{y}(p)$
1	$\dfrac{1}{p}$
k	$\dfrac{k}{p}$
$\sin at$	$\dfrac{a}{p^2+a^2}$
$\cos at$	$\dfrac{p}{p^2+a^2}$
e^{at}	$\dfrac{1}{p-a}$
$\dfrac{t^{n-1}}{(n-1)!}$	$\dfrac{1}{p^n}$

laws for combining impedances. The value of the generalized impedance of a circuit element may be obtained by replacing $(j\omega)$ whenever it occurs in a.c. impedances by p where ω is the angular frequency for sinusoidal operation. Some impedance values Z and the corresponding values of generalized impedance $Z(p)$ for simple circuit elements, and combinations of circuit elements, are given below in Fig. 3.8.

It is now convenient to consider the general case which is illustrated in Fig. 3.9. Consider an impedance $Z_i(p)$ at the input to an operational

FIG. 3.8. Table of simple impedances Z with values of generalized impedances $Z(p)$

Circuit Element	Impedance Z	Generalized Impedance $Z(p)$
 R (resistor)	R	R
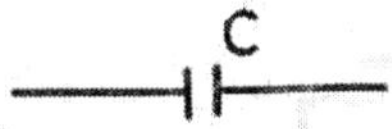 C (capacitor)	$\dfrac{1}{j\omega C}$	$\dfrac{1}{Cp}$
 L (inductor)	$j\omega L$	Lp
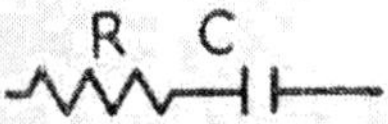 R C (series)	$Z = R + \dfrac{1}{j\omega C}$	$Z(p) = R + \dfrac{1}{pC}$
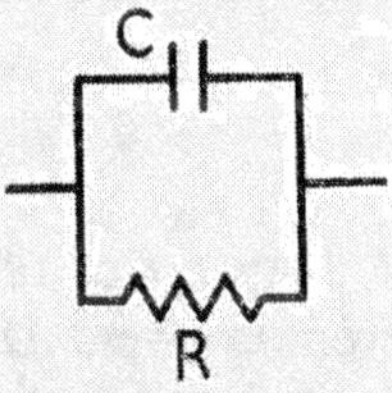 C parallel R	$\dfrac{1}{Z} = \dfrac{1}{R} + \dfrac{1}{1/j\omega C}$ $Z = \dfrac{R}{1 + j\omega CR}$	$Z(p) = \dfrac{R}{1 + pCR}$

amplifier, and an impedance $Z_f(p)$ across the amplifier. Assuming that no grid current flows

$$\bar{\imath}_{in} = \bar{\imath}_f \qquad\qquad \cdot\ 3.19$$

where $\bar{\imath}_{in}$ and $\bar{\imath}_f$ are the Laplace transforms of i_{in} and i_f. If point A is assumed to be at earth potential, and if $\bar{v}_i$ and $\bar{v}_o$ are the transforms of v_i and v_o, then substitution in eqn. 3.19 gives the familiar relation

$$\frac{\bar{v}_o}{\bar{v}_i} \simeq -\frac{Z_f(p)}{Z_i(p)} \qquad\qquad 3.20$$

but now for transformed quantities.

The use of the Laplace transforms in eqn. 3.20 avoids any restriction on the form of input voltage v_i. If non-transformed quantities

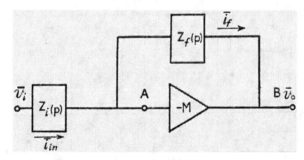

FIG. 3.9. The operational amplifier in the general case

had been used, with impedances expressed in terms of $(j\omega)$, then relation 3.30 would have been valid only for sinusoidal inputs. This would prove a very serious restriction.

3.9 Transfer functions

The idea of transfer function is illustrated by the diagrams of Fig. 3.10. At (a) a simple network of two series resistors is given. The transfer function for a network is the ratio of output to input. In this case, the ratio of output voltage V_o, to input voltage V_i, where the voltages are d.c. quantities. The transfer function is given by the relation

$$\frac{V_o}{V_i} = \frac{R_2}{R_1 + R_2}$$

where the resistances act as a potential divider.

At (b) a resistor and capacitor are connected in series, and a sinusoidal input voltage v_i yields an output sinusoidal voltage v_o. They are related by the transfer function

$$\frac{v_o}{v_i} = \frac{1/j\omega C}{R+1/j\omega C} = \frac{1}{1+j\omega CR}$$

using the method of the j notation.

In Fig. 3.10(c) while the same circuit is employed, no restriction is placed on the shape of the input waveform. The Laplace transform

(a) d.c. input:

$$\frac{V_0}{V_i} = \frac{R_2}{R_1+R_2}$$

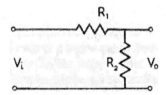

(b) Sinusoidal input:

$$\frac{v_0}{v_i} = \frac{1/j\omega C}{R+1/j\omega C} = \frac{1}{1+j\omega CR}$$

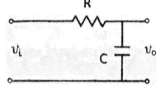

(c) Any input:

$$\frac{\bar{v}_0}{\bar{v}_i} = \frac{1/pC}{R+1/pC} = \frac{1}{1+pCR}$$

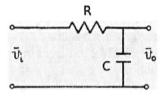

(d) General case:

$$\frac{\bar{v}_0}{\bar{v}_i} = G(p)$$

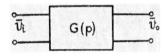

FIG. 3.10. Simple examples of transfer functions

of the input voltage v_i and the output voltage v_o are related by the transfer function,

$$\frac{\bar{v}_o}{\bar{v}_i} = \frac{1/pC}{R+1/pC} = \frac{1}{1+pCR}$$

In the general case shown in Fig. 3.10(d), the network is specified merely as some function $G(p)$ of p. The network is assumed to be linear. The transfer function is given by

$$\frac{\bar{v}_o}{\bar{v}_i} = G(p) \qquad\qquad 3.21$$

An operational amplifier connected as shown in Fig. 3.9 may be used to represent a system having a transfer function $G(p)$ provided suitable input and feedback impedances are employed. Some possible arrangements are shown in Fig. 3.11 as detailed below.

Figure 3.11(a) shows the role of the operational amplifier for sign change. This yields a transfer function

$$\frac{\bar{v}_o}{\bar{v}_i} = -\frac{Z_f(p)}{Z_i(p)}$$

where $\qquad Z_f(p) = Z_i(p) = R$

hence $\qquad \dfrac{\bar{v}_o}{\bar{v}_i} = -\dfrac{R}{R} = -1 \ \ \text{or} \ \ G(p) = -1$

as already seen in Section 3.2.

Figure 3.11(b) indicates integration of an input signal. The transfer function is

$$\frac{\bar{v}_o}{\bar{v}_i} = -\frac{Z_f(p)}{Z_i(p)}$$

where $\qquad Z_f(p) = \dfrac{1}{pC}$

and $\qquad Z_i(p) = R$

Hence $$\frac{\bar{v}_o}{\bar{v}_i} = -\frac{1}{pCR} = -\frac{1}{pT} \quad \text{for} \quad RC = T$$

or $$\bar{v}_o = -\bar{v}_i \frac{1}{T} \cdot \frac{1}{p}$$

This is equivalent to $v_o = -(1/T) \int v_i dt$ from eqn. 3.17 of Section 3.6. Thus $1/p$ in the notation of the Laplace transformation indicates an integration.

Figure 3.11(c) illustrates differentiation

$$\frac{\bar{v}_o}{\bar{v}_i} = -\frac{Z_f(p)}{Z_i(p)}$$

where $$Z_f(p) = R$$

and $$Z_i(p) = \frac{1}{pC}$$

Hence $$\frac{\bar{v}_o}{\bar{v}_i} = -pCR = -pT \quad \text{for} \quad T = RC$$

or $$\bar{v}_o = -Tp\bar{v}_i$$

Now an operational amplifier with a capacitor at input and resistor as a feedback element may be shown to perform differentiation of an input voltage. Hence

$$v_o = -T\frac{d}{dt}(v_i)$$

Thus it is seen on comparing the transformed and untransformed equations above, that p represents a differentiation in the notation of the Laplace transformation just as $1/p$ indicates integration. The use of an operational amplifier connected for differentiation is avoided as far as possible due to practical limitations. Consider, for example, a differentiator to which is applied an input voltage with a content of ripple and noise. As a result of differentiation the output ripple and noise level will be very considerably increased. The design of operational amplifiers capable of differentiation also presents special difficulties connected with amplifier stability.

Figure 3.11(d) shows the effect of using a feedback network consisting of a capacitor and resistor in parallel.

As before

$$\frac{\bar{v}_o}{\bar{v}_i} = -\frac{Z_f(p)}{Z_i(p)}$$

Now $\qquad Z_f(p) = \dfrac{R_2}{1+pC_2R_2} \quad$ and $\quad Z_i(p) = R_1$

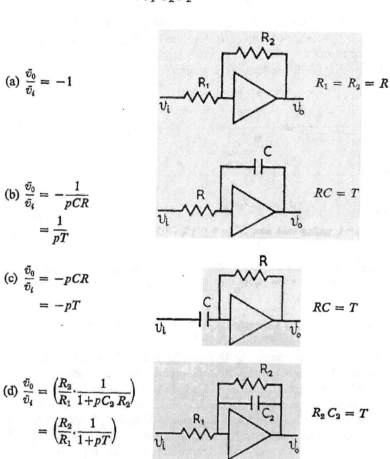

(a) $\dfrac{\bar{v}_0}{\bar{v}_i} = -1$ $\qquad\qquad\qquad\qquad\qquad\qquad\qquad R_1 = R_2 = R$

(b) $\dfrac{\bar{v}_0}{\bar{v}_i} = -\dfrac{1}{pCR}$ $\qquad\qquad\qquad\qquad\qquad\qquad RC = T$

$\qquad = \dfrac{1}{pT}$

(c) $\dfrac{\bar{v}_0}{\bar{v}_i} = -pCR$ $\qquad\qquad\qquad\qquad\qquad\qquad RC = T$

$\qquad = -pT$

(d) $\dfrac{\bar{v}_0}{\bar{v}_i} = \left(\dfrac{R_2}{R_1} \cdot \dfrac{1}{1+pC_2R_2}\right)$ $\qquad\qquad\qquad R_2C_2 = T$

$\qquad = \left(\dfrac{R_2}{R_1} \cdot \dfrac{1}{1+pT}\right)$

FIG. 3.11. Some simple Transfer functions

Hence
$$\frac{\bar{v}_o}{\bar{v}_i} = -\frac{R_2}{R_1}\times\frac{1}{1+pC_2R_2} = -\frac{R_2}{R_1}\times\frac{1}{1+pT}$$

where $C_2R_2 = T$.

The simulation of more ambitious transfer functions using an operational amplifier is illustrated by the examples given in Fig. 3.12. Ref. 3.2 carries the subject considerably further.

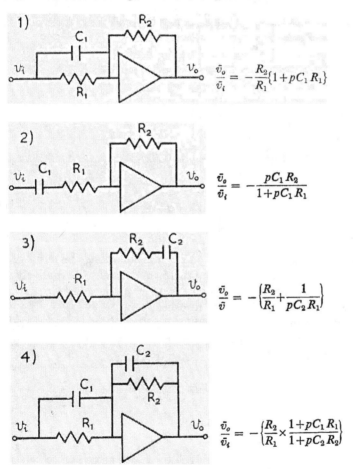

1)
$$\frac{\bar{v}_o}{\bar{v}_i} = -\frac{R_2}{R_1}\{1+pC_1R_1\}$$

2)
$$\frac{\bar{v}_o}{\bar{v}_i} = -\frac{pC_1R_2}{1+pC_1R_1}$$

3)
$$\frac{\bar{v}_o}{\bar{v}} = -\left(\frac{R_2}{R_1}+\frac{1}{pC_2R_1}\right)$$

4)
$$\frac{\bar{v}_o}{\bar{v}_i} = -\left(\frac{R_2}{R_1}\times\frac{1+pC_1R_1}{1+pC_2R_2}\right)$$

FIG. 3.12. Further transfer functions

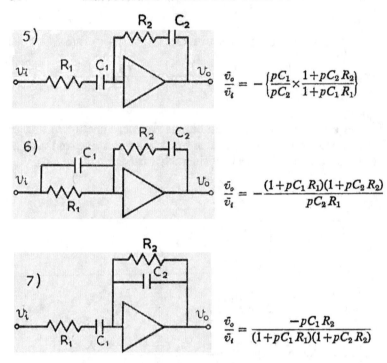

$$\frac{\bar{v}_o}{\bar{v}_i} = -\left\{\frac{pC_1}{pC_2} \times \frac{1+pC_2 R_2}{1+pC_1 R_1}\right\}$$

$$\frac{\bar{v}_o}{\bar{v}_i} = -\frac{(1+pC_1 R_1)(1+pC_2 R_2)}{pC_2 R_1}$$

$$\frac{\bar{v}_o}{\bar{v}_i} = \frac{-pC_1 R_2}{(1+pC_1 R_1)(1+pC_2 R_2)}$$

Fig. 3.12. Continued

3.10 Approach to the solution of equations

In considering the solution of differential equations, the terms of the equation may be written in the form dx^n/dt^n. Alternatively the Laplace notation may be used where p^n replaces d^n/dt^n and $1/p$ represents an integration with respect to time.

In the second case it is essential to replace all time varying quantities, for example, input and output voltages, by their Laplace transforms. Thus for example, a step function

$$y(t) = k$$

becomes

$$\bar{y}(p) = \frac{k}{p}$$

A sinusoidal input

$$y(t) = v = V_{\max} \sin \omega t$$

becomes

$$\bar{y}(p) = V_{\max} \frac{\omega}{p^2 + \omega^2}$$

The Laplace transform is employed extensively, particularly when the analogue computer is used to provide a simulation of the various sections of a linear physical system, in order to replace differential equations involving time by algebraic equations involving p. The use of p functions coupled with the transfer function approach is particularly valuable, for example, in the analysis of the performance of servomechanism systems. Its use with the analogue computer provides a method of setting up problems which is alternative to the direct use of differential equations.

REFERENCES

3.1. JAEGER, J. C. *An Introduction to the Laplace Transformation*, Methuen, London, 1955.
3.2. WALKER, F. *Control*, 3, July p. 100 and August p. 113, 1960.

CHAPTER 4

The Electronic Analogue Machine

4.1 Introduction

In Chapter 3 the use of high gain direct-coupled amplifiers for sign change, addition, and integration was considered. In this chapter their interconnection to solve problems is considered. The basic principle of operation is illustrated by the solution of a simple second-order equation. Machine control and procedures for setting up a desired operating configuration are discussed in some detail.

4.2 Solution of a second-order equation

The behaviour of many physical systems may be represented by a second-order differential equation of the form

$$a\frac{d^2y}{dt^2}+b\frac{dy}{dt}+cy = f(t) \qquad\qquad 4.1(a)$$

Such an equation defines, for example, the acceleration, velocity, and position of a mass moving in accordance with Newton's Second Law of motion – force equals mass multiplied by acceleration – under the influence of a frictional force proportional to velocity, an elastic restoring force proportional to displacement, and an externally applied force $f(t)$. A more concise method of representation might be,

$$a\ddot{y}+b\dot{y}+cy = f(t) \qquad\qquad 4.1(b)$$

In attempting to solve such an equation it is usually convenient to rewrite eqn. 4.1(b) with the highest derivative term on the left-hand side. Thus

$$a\ddot{y} = f(t)-b\dot{y}-cy \qquad\qquad 4.1(c)$$

Initially the presence of the term $a\ddot{y}$ is assumed. The term $a\ddot{y}$ is applied to the input of an integrator whose output is taken as $-b\dot{y}$ to some convenient scale. A second integration yields $+cy$. The sign reversals are inherent in the integration. Figure 4.1 indicates the

38

arrangement. So far the system is in a similar condition to the arrangement used by Kelvin when endeavouring to solve a similar equation mechanically. As in his case the aim is now to generate the sum of the terms on the right-hand side of equation 4.1(c). Connection of the sum to the input of the first integrator constrains the arrangement to solve continuously the equation of 4.1(c).

This closed-loop system is shown in Fig. 4.2. A sign-reversing amplifier is connected into the loop to provide the correct sign for the term in $\dot{y}$. $f(t)$ may be any function of t. In a typical case $f(t)$ may be a step function or a sinusoidal signal. The output may be taken at any convenient place. The variation of y with time is frequently

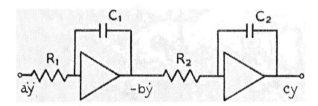

FIG. 4.1. Block schematic of double integration

required when the recording equipment would be connected at point A in Fig. 4.2. The form of the recording equipment would depend on the time taken for the parameters of the problem to settle down to their steady-state values. In many cases a pen recorder may be used. If the steady-state is reached quickly, then a cathode-ray tube display photographically recorded may be preferred. With multi-channel recording equipment the behaviour of several quantities with time may be examined. For the problem under consideration, for example, cy, $b\dot{y}$, and $a\ddot{y}$ may all be sampled continuously at points A, B, and C of Fig. 4.2.

Alternatively the problem might have been stated in the form

$$ap^2 y + bpy + cy = \bar{f}(p) \qquad\qquad 4.1(\text{d})$$

where p has the significance discussed in the last chapter. $\bar{f}(p)$ is the transform of $f(t)$. Exactly the same configuration of operational amplifiers would be employed for the solution.

4.3 Machine control and insertion of initial values

In the simple case considered in the last section, no mention was made of the control of the computer. Machine operation is normally

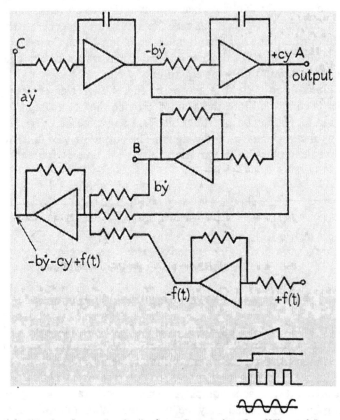

FIG. 4.2. Block schematic of solution of second-order differential equation

$$a\ddot{y}+b\dot{y}+cy = f(t)$$

controlled by relays which determine the state of the machine. Three or four states of operation are normal.

1. *Zero set (Z.S.) condition.* This is the initial state of the machine after switch-on. In this condition the input resistors of all the operational amplifiers are earthed. Resistors are applied across feedback capacitors to ensure that they are discharged.

Every operational amplifier is normally provided with a potentiometer adjustment by which the output voltage may be set equal to
zero when the input voltage is zero. The process is known as 'zero
setting'. The frequency with which zero setting is required is a measure
of the quality of the operational amplifiers used in the machine. Drift
in the amplifier is the reason for the necessity of such adjustment.
Causes of drift and methods of reducing it are discussed later.

While with early amplifiers frequent balancing was required, drift

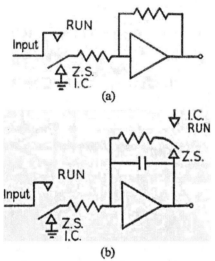

FIG. 4.3. Zero setting arrangements. (a) Sign change. (b) Integration.
Initial condition arrangements omitted

rates are now so low with modern amplifiers that adjustment is only
made at the beginning of each working period, say each day. Neon
warning lamps are usually fitted to the front panel of each amplifier
to indicate the incidence of unbalance. Frequently the neon lamp also
serves to indicate overload conditions at the amplifier output.

Typical zero setting arrangements are shown in Fig. 4.3.

2. *Initial conditions (I.C.)*. It may happen that it is necessary to
provide initial values at integrators. The method is illustrated in
Fig. 4.4 which shows an operational amplifier connected to an
integrator with relays arranged for initial conditions. A voltage $-v$

4

is applied via an auxiliary input resistor R_a. This produces an output voltage $v_{o(t=0)}$ and provides the feedback capacitor with its initial charge. In this condition the operational amplifier is being used as a scale change amplifier. The presence of the feedback capacitor C, however, requires that the computer must remain in the 'initial

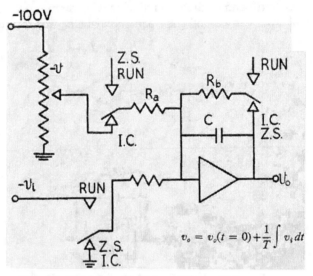

FIG. 4.4. Provision of initial conditions at integrators

conditions' state sufficiently long for the capacitor to be charged through $v_{o(t=0)}$ volts. In the steady state

$$v_{o(t=0)} = v\left(\frac{R_b}{R_a}\right)$$

On energizing the relays, the run condition is achieved. The operational amplifier is connected as an integrator having an initial charge $v_{o(t=0)}$. The auxiliary circuit is disconnected. An input voltage $-v_i$ yields an output voltage v_o given by,

$$v_o = v_{o(t=0)} + \frac{1}{T}\int v_i\, dt \qquad\qquad 4.2$$

3. *Run condition.* In the run condition all the operational amplifiers used in the problem are interconnected and the solution proceeds for as long as the operator wishes. For the case of the second-order system discussed in the previous section, the solution will frequently settle down to a steady value. Once this has been reached, the machine operator has normally no further interest in the problem. The machine is then restored to either the 'zero set' condition if it is necessary to check for drift, or more usually to the 'initial condition' state when different initial values and different coefficients can be inserted in the problem.

4. *Hold (freeze).* In some cases it is desirable to hold the values achieved at the end of a run for some little time before returning to the initial conditions state for the next run. In the hold condition, integrator inputs are earthed resulting in their outputs remaining at a constant value. This feature allows the machine operator to read off final values at leisure. Provision may also be made for the 'hold' state to occur conditional upon some other parameter or parameters. In a computation concerning the flight of an anti-aircraft shell, for example, the 'hold' state would occur whenever the distance between target and shell became equal to the range at which the proximity fuse became effective.

4.4 Machine interconnection

In early electronic analogue computers, interconnection between the various operational amplifiers tended to be via wander leads connected to tag-strips at the rear of the amplifiers themselves. For scale changing and addition, computing resistors were selected, measured with a Wheatstone bridge and augmented as necessary with resistors of low value to ensure that resistor ratios were within the tolerances permitted by the problem under consideration. Since the resistors used in computing are frequently of the order of 1 MΩ, some considerable skill is required in this time consuming task. Capacitors used for integration were carefully measured. Typical values might be 0·1 μF to 1 μF. The correct time constants were achieved by providing resistors which when augmented as mentioned above gave a value of T which was within the limits set by the desired accuracy of the problem. After measurement the circuit elements were usually soldered into place, with the possibility of values changing due to the heating of components.

Such techniques made for a comparatively inflexible system in which considerable time and effort would be required to change the problem on the machine. Since many of the early analogue computers were in fact built specially as simulators of specific systems, usually aircraft or guided weapon systems, the restriction was not as serious as might have been supposed. A problem might remain on the machine for many months. Many test runs would be performed with different coefficient values. Sub-sections of the overall problem would be modified and enlarged from time to time. Sections of the problem represented to a first approximation by simple transfer functions would be represented later by more ambitious transfer functions. Items of the physical system under consideration might be included, particularly if they behaved in a manner which would be difficult to simulate accurately. Eventually a large machine of perhaps more than a hundred operational amplifiers, and having a considerable number of electromechanical axis transformation units, would result.

In time, however, it was appreciated that there would be considerable scope for comparatively small analogue computers which were general purpose machines, provided that a large variety of completely different problems could be set up with ease. The principal features which distinguish such machines from the earlier ones are outlined below. These general purpose analogue machines are now in wide use.

The inputs and output of each operational amplifier or other computing element are brought out to sockets at an interconnection or 'patch' panel at the front of the machine. Schematic diagrams on this panel are so arranged that the function of each element may be seen at a glance. A section of a typical patch panel is shown in Fig. 4.5. In this case the computing elements are already in position. Sometimes the user inserts them. Normally several input sockets are available to permit more than one input voltage to each operational amplifier. Several output sockets are connected in parallel at the output of the operational amplifier. This enables more than one output connection to be made. In certain cases the summing point is also brought out to a socket at the patch panel. Sockets are frequently colour coded for easy identification. Short wander leads are used for interconnection.

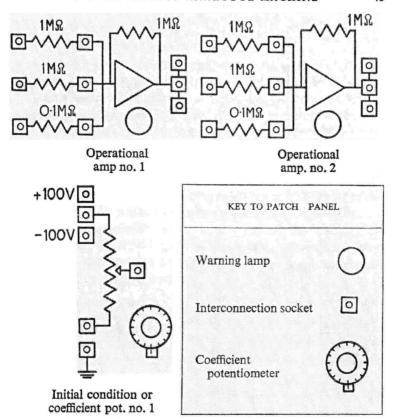

FIG. 4.5. Section of patch panel of typical general-purpose machine

In some cases provision is made for the removal of the complete patch panel with the interconnections appropriate to a particular problem, and the substitution of other patch panels with the correct connections for further problems already made. In this way a library of solution arrangements can be built up.

4.5 Setting-up procedures

(i) *At the operational amplifier.* Measurement of components is eliminated as far as possible. Integrators normally have fixed values of feedback capacitor, say two values, and a choice of several values of input resistor. With sign change, scale change, and addition, a fixed value of feedback resistor R_f and a choice of several values of

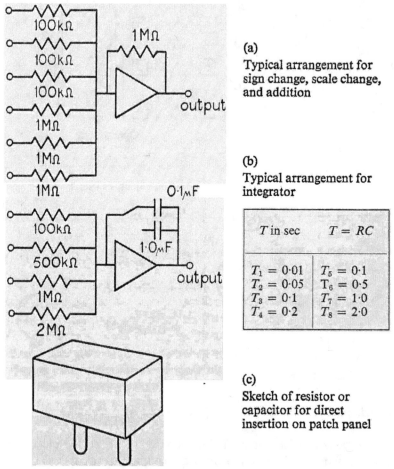

(a)

Typical arrangement for sign change, scale change, and addition

(b)

Typical arrangement for integrator

T in sec	$T = RC$
$T_1 = 0.01$	$T_5 = 0.1$
$T_2 = 0.05$	$T_6 = 0.5$
$T_3 = 0.1$	$T_7 = 1.0$
$T_4 = 0.2$	$T_8 = 2.0$

(c)

Sketch of resistor or capacitor for direct insertion on patch panel

Fig. 4.6. Typical practical values for operational amplifiers

input resistor are normally available and in many cases are already wired into position behind the panel. Selection is frequently made by switching. Arrangements with typical practical values are shown in Fig. 4.6. The relays associated with machine operation are omitted for the sake of simplicity.

Figure 4.6(a) shows an operational amplifier for scale change or addition. Six inputs are available, three of 0·1 MΩ, and three of 1·0 MΩ. Thus a maximum of six inputs can be accommodated. In this case addition would be accompanied by three gains of (− 10) and three gains of (− 1). If the arrangement of the patch panel permits, it may be possible to arrange two or more input resistors in parallel so that further values of gain are available. For example two resistors of 1 MΩ in parallel would provide a gain of (−2).

At Fig. 4.6(b) a typical integrator is shown. Two capacitor values are available 0·1 μF and 1·0 μF. Four input resistors are provided. The various combinations of resistance and capacitance permit seven values of time constant if one input is used. Up to four inputs at one time are possible so that summation with integration is possible.

In small machines where space is very limited, the resistors and capacitors used in a particular problem take standard values as mentioned above, but are inserted directly at the patch panel as required by the machine operator. This technique is illustrated in Fig. 4.6(c).

High stability, close tolerance components are used to ensure good accuracy. As has already been mentioned, computing accuracy with modern machines depends to a very considerable extent on the ratio of resistors in scale change and addition, and the value of time constants for integrators. A typical tolerance for resistor values is 0·1 per cent and for capacitors 0·5 or 0·1 per cent. The trend is towards even more close tolerances on component values. In some computers, for example, resistors and capacitors are enclosed in temperature-controlled ovens to ensure that values do not change significantly with variation of ambient temperature. In many cases the accuracy achieved with the above methods will suffice. If greater precision is required, various bridge methods may be used.

(ii) *Coefficient potentiometers*. Gain change other than by fixed values is achieved at coefficient potentiometers. In early computers potentiometers with the resistance track wound on a multi-turn helix were freely used for this purpose. Ten-turn potentiometers were typical. The calibrated potentiometer dial was divided into one hundred divisions, and since ten complete revolutions were available, slider positions could be set up to one part in a thousand quite easily.

Typically these potentiometers were linear to within 0·1 per cent. They represented a very considerable advance on potentiometers capable of rotation through 270° only. They were expensive, and for accurate work had to be used with caution. For example, consider the

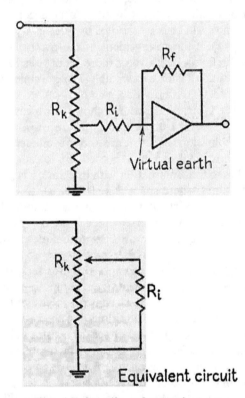

Virtual earth

Equivalent circuit

FIG. 4.7. Loading of potentiometer

case of a coefficient potentiometer, the slider of which is connected to the input resistance of an operational amplifier. Such an arrangement is illustrated in Fig. 4.7. The input resistor R_i shunts the lower portion of the helical potentiometer. Unless allowance is made for this, a potentiometer set to the value of coefficient required would give a lower value than the correct one because of the loading by the input resistor. Families of curves showing the effect of loading coefficient potentiometers for different values of potentiometer resistance R_k and input resistance R_l were used to overcome this difficulty. In order to minimize loadings, R_k should be as small as possible compared with R_l. The limit to the value of R_k is normally set by the maximum current which R_k is permitted to pass.

Recently, more economical methods have been used. Lower quality potentiometers, not always multi-turn, have been employed in

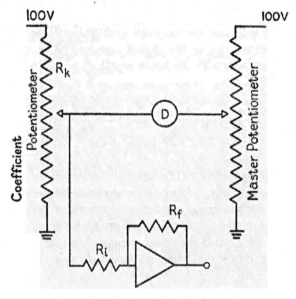

FIG. 4.8. Balancing procedure

association with a master potentiometer. A typical arrangement is shown in Fig. 4.8. The slider of the coefficient potentiometer is connected to the input resistor of the operational amplifier R_l. The master potentiometer is set to the precise value of coefficient required. Standard reference voltages of the same magnitude, say $+100$ V are applied to the top of each potentiometer. The sliders of each are connected via a galvanometer. The slider of the coefficient potentiometer is adjusted until a null is indicated on the galvanometer. In this condition no current passes through the meter, and the presence of the master potentiometer has no effect on the remainder of the circuit. Relays are used to connect the reference voltages and measuring equipment temporarily into circuit.

As an alternative, a digital voltmeter may be used to monitor the voltage at the slider of the potentiometer when the input resistor R_i is connected. This is a device with a very high input impedance. Its shunting effect may normally be neglected. Digital voltmeters are capable of direct read-out to one part in 1000 or even 10,000. Since the voltage they measure is displayed in the form of numerals it may be employed with ease by relatively unskilled personnel. With the increasing general use of the digital voltmeter such a method is attractive, especially with the larger machines where its high cost is more justifiable.

In cases where great precision is required in the setting up of operational amplifiers as scale changers or adders, bridge methods involving the operational amplifier itself may be used. One such is described in Ref. 4.1.

(iii) *Initial conditions.* The method is illustrated in Fig. 4.4 and has been discussed in Section 4.3. The voltage $-v$ set in from the potentiometer may be checked using the master potentiometer technique mentioned above. If very considerable precision is required, the bridge methods which incorporate the operational amplifier itself may be used. In many machines positive and negative reference voltages which are highly stable are used to provide the potentials for the insertion of initial conditions. Such reference voltages are typically of the order of ± 100 volts.

(iv) *Step function input.* Such a function is frequently required. The step function input voltage may be derived from the same reference source as the voltages used to provide the initial conditions at the integrators. The magnitude of the step function voltage may be determined in a similar manner.

4.6 Time scales
In many cases operation will be in real time. This is particularly the case when the computer is in use as a simulator of physical systems of the servo mechanism, or aircraft, type. In some cases, however, it may be desirable to work with 'scaled' time.

When the time scale is such that the computation is concluded within a few seconds or less, facilities for the use of the machine in a repetitive role may be valuable. Long persistence cathode-ray tube displays may be used in conjunction with cameras to record the results.

Some machines have precise time measuring facilities. Provision is made for continuous repetition of the control sequence, zero set, initial conditions, run. Computing periods range from 0·1 seconds to 20 seconds for example.

4.7 Scaling of a problem

The process by which a problem is set on an analogue computer may be divided into two sections.

First it is necessary to decide upon the appropriate configuration of computing elements which will represent the physical system correctly. The basis of this procedure has been discussed already.

The second consideration is the determination of the operational amplifier gains, of coefficient potentiometer settings, and of suitable values for the scale factors applied to the voltages which represent the variables of the physical system. These must be such as to yield the correct numerical solution to the problem. This second consideration is known as scaling of the problem. It is of considerable importance. Before scaling a problem a number of factors must be taken into consideration.

The first is the value of the maximum voltage available at the output of an operational amplifier for linear operation. This voltage swing determines the largest signal voltage which may be employed. Its value depends on the amplifier design. For valve amplifiers where the H.T. supplies are of the order of plus and minus 300 volts, typical maximum values of voltage swing are plus and minus 100 volts provided only small currents are drawn from the output of the amplifier. The voltage swing will diminish if larger currents are taken. A typical plot of load versus swing is shown in Fig. 4.9. It indicates that it is important to ensure that the value of load resistance is kept within reasonable limits. This load resistance frequently takes the form of a set of coefficient potentiometers arranged in parallel, and used for subsequent sections of the problem. The ohmic value, and number of such potentiometers must always be a compromise between the demands of the computer configuration and the need to keep the total potentiometer loading such that the current drawn is not too high. If the ohmic value of the individual potentiometers is too large, however, then the application of computing resistors at their sliders

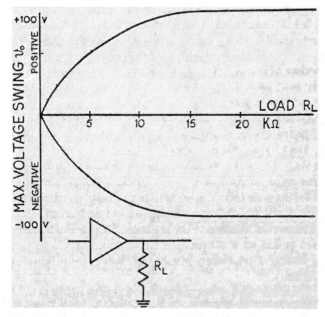

FIG. 4.9. Graph showing effect of load resistance on maximum output voltage swing

may result in an excessive shunting effect as discussed in Section 4.5(ii).

A second important consideration is that of the possible maximum values of the various terms in the equation representing the problem. In many cases these may be known, at least approximately. In an aircraft problem, for example, the maximum velocity and acceleration of which the plane is capable will be known. In other cases a reasonable guess at the maximum values may often be made.

In the interests of an accurate solution, it is desirable to keep the voltages which represent the various physical quantities of the problem as large as is compatible with the danger of overloading the operational amplifiers. When very small voltages represent the quantities, drift voltages and noise may be of comparable magnitude, with the result that the accuracy of the solution falls off. With modern machines such difficulties would only become serious if the signal voltages are considerably less than one volt.

In practice a first attempt at scaling a problem may not prove completely satisfactory. Overload at some of the operational amplifiers would be indicated by the overload warning lamps. After rescaling various sections of the problem as necessary, a further run would be tried. The presence of very small voltages in the system might be investigated next. Finally after several trials, the first of the series of actual runs would be performed. In many problems the coefficients of the various terms will have a range of values. Scaling of the problem must take account of this range of values.

In order to illustrate some of the problems, scaling of the equation to a second-order system similar to that discussed in Section 4.2 will now be considered.

Equation 4.3(a) represents the response of a second-order system with damping to an input signal

$$\ddot{\theta}_o + 2\zeta\omega\dot{\theta}_o + \omega^2\theta_o = \theta_i \qquad \qquad 4.3(a)$$

where ω_o = undamped natural angular frequency of the system in rad/sec

ζ = damping ratio

θ_i = input step function in radians

θ_o = output signal in radians.

Such systems are frequently encountered in servomechanism work. See, for example, Ref. 4.2. It is well known that the response of such a system to a step function input depends on the value of the damping ratio ζ. For $\zeta = 0$, the system is oscillatory with peak-to-peak amplitude equal to twice the input step. As the value of ζ rises to unity the response becomes progressively more damped, with fewer overshoots before reaching the steady-state value where $\theta_o = \theta_i$. At $\zeta = 1$, the critical value of damping occurs when the output rises to a value equal to the input step without any overshoot. When $\zeta > 1$, the response becomes increasingly sluggish.

Initially it is convenient to rewrite the equation with the highest derivative only on the left-hand side.

$$\ddot{\theta}_o = \theta_i - 2\zeta\omega\dot{\theta}_o - \omega^2\theta_o \qquad \qquad 4.3(\text{b})$$

A computer configuration similar to that shown in Fig. 4.2 is suitable for the solution of such a second-order system, though in practice some reduction in the number of amplifiers required could be achieved.

In order to use the machine to best advantage, some idea of the maximum values of the various terms in the equation must first be obtained. The maximum value of θ_o will be twice the input step θ_i. This occurs when $\zeta = 0$. In this condition the system is oscillatory, behaving as a simple harmonic motion with period

$$T = \frac{2\pi}{\omega} \sec$$

The maximum value of $\dot{\theta}_o$ will be $\omega\theta_i$ and the maximum value of $\ddot{\theta}_o$ will be $\omega^2\theta_i$. Suppose for the sake of simplicity that the undamped natural frequency ω_o is one rad/sec, and that θ_i, the input step function is equal to one rad.

The equation then becomes

$$\ddot{\theta}_o = 1 - 2\zeta\dot{\theta}_o - \theta_o \qquad \qquad 4.3(\text{c})$$

Suppose we wish to investigate the solution to the problem for a range of values of damping ratio from $\zeta = 0$ to $\zeta = 2$. Figure 4.10 shows a computer configuration suitable for the solution of eqn. 4.3(c). Scaling or component values are not shown.

In setting up the solution to the above problem, various methods of approach are possible. The gain of the operational amplifiers, the setting of coefficient potentiometers, and the scales adopted for the analogue voltages are all inter-related. Initially it is convenient to consider them separately as far as possible, though this may not always make for the best use of the machine.

(i) *Gains of operational amplifiers.* First suppose that the same scaling will be used throughout the problem if this can be arranged. One volt will represent a units of $\ddot{\theta}_o$, $\dot{\theta}_o$, θ_o, and θ_i if possible. Now take the

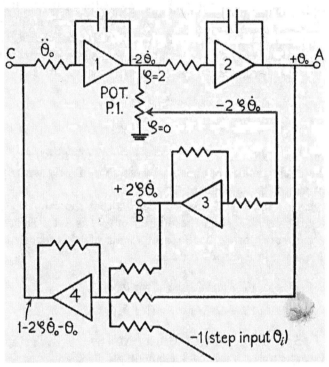

FIG. 4.10. Block diagram of computer configuration to solve eqn. 4.3(c)
$$\ddot{\theta}_0 + 2\zeta\dot{\theta}_0 + \theta_0 = 1$$

operational amplifiers in turn and consider the gain they must have to satisfy Eqn. 4.3(c). First consider an operational amplifier used for integration. The input voltage v_i and output voltage v_o are related as follows

$$v_o = -\frac{1}{T}\int_0^t v_i\,dt$$

Hence $1/T$ may be considered as the gain of the operational amplifier. If $1/T$ equalled unity, for example, there would be an output of 1 volt/sec for a steady input of 1 volt. If $1/T = 10$, there would be an output of 10 volt/sec for a steady input of 1 volt. Now take the first integration of the problem under consideration.

Operational amplifier 1. It is seen from Fig. 4.10 that an output $-2\ddot{\theta}_o$ is required for an input $+\ddot{\theta}_o$. If the scales for $\ddot{\theta}_o$ and $\dot{\theta}_o$ are to be the same, a gain of 2 will be required at the operational amplifier. Thus if 1 volt represents a rad/sec^2 for $\ddot{\theta}_o$, then the scale for $\dot{\theta}_o$ will have the same numerical value of 1 volt represents a rad/sec where a is the scale factor. A convenient method of representation is

$$1V \sim a \text{ rad/sec}^2 \quad (\text{for } \ddot{\theta}_o)$$

$$1V \sim a \text{ rad/sec} \quad (\text{for } \dot{\theta}_o)$$

The gain of 2 would be achieved if, for example, the resistor at the input to the operational amplifier had a value of 1 MΩ when the feedback capacitor had a value of 0·5 μF.

Operational amplifier 2. Figure 4.10 shows that the input to the second integrator is $-2\dot{\theta}_o$ and the desired output is $+\theta_o$. Hence if the scales for $\dot{\theta}_o$ and θ_o are to be the same, a gain of 0·5 is required.

The scales at the integrator would be

$$1V \sim a \text{ rad/sec} \quad (\text{for } \dot{\theta}_o)$$

$$1V \sim a \text{ rad.} \quad (\text{for } \theta_o)$$

The gain of 0·5 would be achieved with a 1 MΩ resistor at the input, and a 2 μF capacitor as a feedback element.

Coefficient potentiometer P.1. It will be seen from Fig. 4.10 that the output of amplifier 1 is $-2\dot{\theta}_o$ while the quantity at the slider of the coefficient potentiometer is $-2\zeta\dot{\theta}_o$. A multiplication by a constant ζ therefore takes place at the potentiometer. Multiplication by a constant less than unity can take place without difficulty at a coefficient potentiometer and no change of scale need occur. In this case however, the maximum value which ζ may take is $\zeta = 2$. The multiplication must therefore take place in the scaling. In order to satisfy the relation shown in Fig. 4.10, 1 volt at the slider of the potentiometer must represent twice as many units of ζ as 1 volt at the output of operational amplifier 1, i.e.

$1V \sim a$ rad/sec at the output of amplifier 1

$1V \sim 2a$ rad/sec at the slider of potentiometer P.1

Operational amplifier 3. A suitable choice of input and feedback resistors at amplifier 3 will enable the scale at its output to be restored to the same value as that throughout the remainder of the problem. If the ratio of output resistor to feedback resistor is set equal to 2, resulting in a gain of 2, then the scale for θ_o at the output of amplifier 3 will have the same value as at the output of amplifier 1, i.e.

$1V \sim 2a$ rad/sec at the input to amplifier 3

$1V \sim a$ rad/sec at the output to amplifier 3

Operational amplifier 4. The scaling applied to the $\dot{\theta}_o$ and θ_o terms at the input to operational amplifier 4 is the same in each case

$1V \sim a$ rad/sec   (for $\dot{\theta}_o$)

$1V \sim a$ rad.   (for θ_o)

If the scale for the input step θ_i has the same value

$1V \sim a$ rad.   (for θ_i)

then summation is achieved if the gain of the three input channels is the same. Unity gain is required to ensure that the scale

$1V \sim a$ rad/sec^2 (for $\ddot{\theta}_o$)

at the output of the summing amplifier is the same as that at the input to operational amplifier 1.

(ii) *Value of scale factor 'a'.* In deciding on the value for the scale factor a, it is desirable to choose a value such that as large an amplifier swing as possible is employed. To do this an approximate knowledge of the maximum values of the variables of the problem is necessary.

5

For the problem under consideration, the maximum values of the variables are as follows:

$$\theta_{i\,max} = 1 \text{ rad.}$$
$$\theta_{o\,max} = 2 \text{ rad.}$$
$$\dot{\theta}_{o\,max} = 1 \text{ rad/sec}$$
$$\ddot{\theta}_{o\,max} = 1 \text{ rad/sec}^2$$
$$\zeta_{max} = 2$$
$$\omega_o = 1 \text{ rad/sec}$$

Consider the operational amplifiers in turn.

Operational amplifier 1. Consider the output of operational amplifier 1. If the maximum swing for linear operation is ± 100 V, then since the output is $-2\dot{\theta}_o$, the maximum possible value of a is $\frac{1}{50}$ when

$$1V \sim \tfrac{1}{50} \text{ rad/sec} \quad (\text{for } \dot{\theta}_o)$$

Operational amplifier 2. At amplifier 2, the same value of scale factor has been assumed with the result that

$$1V \sim \tfrac{1}{50} \text{ rad.} \quad (\text{for } \theta_o)$$

This is acceptable since the maximum value of θ_o is 2 radians which would give a maximum value of ± 100 V at the output of the amplifier.

Potentiometer P.1. The top of the potentiometer is taken as representing $\zeta = 2$. Hence for a maximum permitted voltage of ± 100 V, we have at the slider

$$100V \sim 2\zeta\dot{\theta}_{o\,max}$$

and for $\dot{\theta}_{o\,max} = 1$ rad/sec and $\zeta = 2$, this yields

$$100V \sim 4 \text{ rad/sec}$$

or
$$1V \sim \tfrac{1}{25} \text{ rad/sec}$$

Thus the scaling at the slider of the potentiometer is $1V \sim 2\alpha$ rad/sec

Operational amplifier 3. The output of amplifier 3 is $+2\zeta\dot{\theta}_o$. If the value $a = \frac{1}{50}$ is used, the maximum theoretical output of the amplifier would rise to 200V which is not possible due to the practical limitations imposed by the amplifier design. This indicates the need for revision of the value of the scale factor a. Before doing this, however, it is useful to consider the final operational amplifier.

Operational amplifier 4. It is important to realize that in general, the output of a summing amplifier may represent the point at which the worst overload may occur. In this particular case, the phase relation of the various terms in the summation

$$\ddot{\theta}_o = 1 - \theta_o - 2\zeta\dot{\theta}_o$$

is such that $\ddot{\theta}_o$ does not rise above 1 rad/sec^2 represented by the scaling 1V $\sim \frac{1}{80}$ rad/sec^2, for which overload does not occur. In general it is safer to assume that all the terms in a summation may have their maximum values, each of the same sign, at the same time.

(iii) *Revised value of scale factor.* In view of the overload at amplifier 3, a more conservative scaling might now be considered. Let a have a value $\frac{1}{10}$. Then the scaling throughout the system is given by the relations below.

Output of amplifier 1:   1V $\sim \frac{1}{10}$ rad/sec

Output of amplifier 2:   1V $\sim \frac{1}{10}$ rad.

At slider of potentiometer P.1:   1V $\sim \frac{1}{5}$ rad/sec

Output of amplifier 3:   1V $\sim \frac{1}{10}$ rad/sec

Input step function: 1V $\sim \frac{1}{10}$ rad.

Figure 4.11 indicates the amplifier configuration for the solution of this problem. Typical values of the computing impedances are shown, as is the scaling.

(iv) *Limitations imposed by equipment available.* Now consider a modification to the arrangement discussed above. In many cases with general purpose computers, the values of the computing impedances which are available are restricted. Consider the case where the feedback element is either a capacitor of 1μF or resistor of 1 MΩ, and the input resistors have values of either 1MΩ or 100 kΩ. These restrictions would result in modification to the computer set-up shown in Fig. 4.11 for the solution of eqn. 4.3(c). The revised arrangement is shown in Fig. 4.12. This indicates the scaling and the values of the resistors and capacitors. The operational amplifiers are considered in turn below.

For amplifier 1 the gain was 2, and is now 1. Hence the form of the equation is retained via the scaling. For a scale of

$$1V \sim \tfrac{1}{10} \text{ rad/sec}^2 \quad \text{(for } \ddot{\theta}_o\text{)}$$

$$1V \sim \tfrac{1}{8} \text{ rad/sec} \quad \text{(for } \dot{\theta}_o\text{)}$$

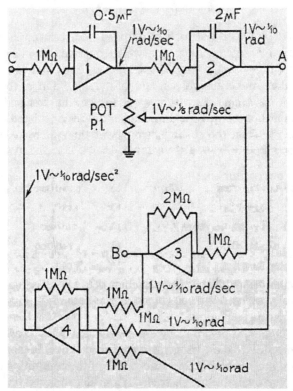

Fig. 4.11. Solution of eqn. 4.3(c) showing values of computing impedances and scaling

This gives the same result as an amplifier gain of 2 with equal scales at input and output.

In the case of amplifier 2 the gain was 0·5 and is now 1. Hence the form of the equation is retained through appropriate scaling. The scaling for θ_o at the input is the same as that at the output of amplifier 1, i.e. $1V \sim \frac{1}{5}$ rad/sec. An effective gain of 0·5 is obtained if the scaling at the output is taken as $1V \sim \frac{1}{10}$ rad.

The output at the slider of the coefficient potentiometer is $-2\zeta\theta_o$

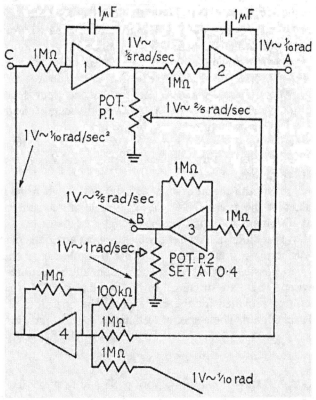

FIG. 4.12. Alternative solution of eqn. 4.3(c) showing modified scaling

as in the previous case. The multiplication by 2 is again provided in the scaling. The input to the potentiometer, $-2\theta_o$, has the same scaling as the output of operational amplifier 1, i.e. $1V \sim \frac{1}{5}$ rad/sec. Hence at the slider $-2\zeta\theta_o$ is represented with the scaling, $1V \sim 2 \times \frac{1}{5}$ rad/sec or $1V \sim \frac{2}{5}$ rad/sec.

For unity gain, the scale at the output to amplifier 3, will be the same as at the input $1V \sim \frac{2}{5}$ rad/sec.

Some care is required when considering the scaling at operational amplifier 4. The scale at the output must correspond to that at the input to amplifier 1, i.e. $1V \sim \frac{1}{10}$ rad/sec^2.

Take the $2\zeta\dot{\theta}_o$ channel first. The scale at the input is $1V \sim \frac{2}{5}$ rad/sec. Insertion of a potentiometer P.2 set at 0·4 where unity represents the top of the potentiometer would mean that 0·4 V at the potentiometer slider would represent $\frac{2}{5}$ rad/sec if 1V at the top indicated $\frac{2}{5}$ rad/sec. Thus at the potentiometer slider $1V \sim 1$ rad/sec. If the gain of the channel was now made equal to 10, the scale at the output of amplifier 4 to satisfy eqn. 4.3(c) would be $1V \sim \frac{1}{10}$ rad/sec^2 as desired.

The θ_o channel is easier to scale. The scale at the input is $1V \sim \frac{1}{10}$ rad. The equation is satisfied with unity gain and a scale at the output of $1V \sim \frac{1}{10}$ rad/sec^2 which is the required value.

Similarly a unit step, to a scale of $1V \sim \frac{1}{10}$ rad., on the third channel having unity gain, and a scale at the output of $1V \sim \frac{1}{10}$ rad/sec^2 satisfies the equation.

A check round the circuit of Fig. 4.12 shows that when the maximum values of the quantities $\ddot{\theta}_o$, $\dot{\theta}_o$, θ_o, and θ_i are considered, no overload of operational amplifiers results.

The above methods used to set problems on an analogue machine prove satisfactory in many cases. In order to exploit a machine to the very best possible advantage, special systematic procedures have been devised. These are discussed in the handbooks of the various manufacturers provided for the guidance of the operators of their particular machines. These special techniques are also mentioned in Ref. 4.3.

REFERENCES

4.1. HARTLEY, M. G. *Control*, 4, April p. 98 and May p. 103, 1961.

4.2. TAYLOR, P. L. *Servomechanisms*, Longmans, London, 1960.

4.3. KORN, G. A., and KORN, T. M. *Electronic Analog Computers* McGraw-Hill, New York, 1956.

Practical d.c. Amplifiers

5.1 Introduction

Chapter 5 gives a brief account of some of the features of valve d.c. amplifiers important for computing applications. The account is of necessity sketchy. A fuller treatment is available in the larger works on analogue computing. In particular the reader is referred to Refs. 5.1 and 5.2. The effects of the departure of amplifier performance from the ideals set out at the beginning of Chapter 3 are considered in some detail.

5.2 Amplification with triode and pentode valves

Valve amplifiers used in analogue computing consist of a number of thermionic triode or pentode valves connected to provide voltage amplification. The operation of a simple amplifying stage is illustrated in Fig. 5.1. At 5.1(a) a schematic diagram of a triode is shown. Thermionic emission from the cathode constitutes a current through the valve, I_a, conventionally flowing from anode to cathode.

The negative voltage V_g, applied to the grid controls the anode current, I_a, as shown by the family of characteristic curves of Fig. 5.1(b). An increase of anode voltage, V_a, produces a corresponding increase of anode current, I_a, for a constant grid voltage. This relation is seen more clearly in Fig. 5.1(c) which gives the family of curves relating anode voltage and anode current for various values of grid voltage. Figure 5.2 shows similar curves for a typical pentode. The change of shape in the characteristic curves of Fig. 5.2(b) and Fig. 5.2(c) are brought about by the action of the additional grids indicated in Fig. 5.2(a).

The amplifying action of a valve stage is illustrated in Fig. 5.3 where a small sinusoidal signal, v_g, is shown applied to the control grid of a triode. A steady current flowing through the cathode bias resistor R_b ensures that operation is with respect to a suitable steady value of grid voltage. The capacitor C_b, in parallel with resistor R_b,

63

has a reactance which is small at signal frequencies and effectively short-circuits R_b to signals. If the excursion of the grid signal about the 'working point' does not extend beyond the linear region of the

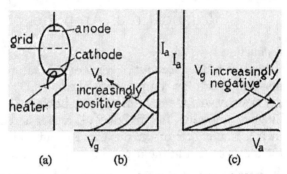

FIG. 5.1. Triode valve. (a) Schematic of triode. (b) and (c) Characteristics of triode

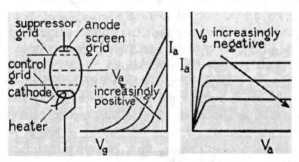

FIG. 5.2. Pentode valve. (a) Schematic of pentode. (b) and (c) Characteristics of pentode

characteristic curve, a sinusoidal variation in anode current, i_a, appears. This sinusoidal current flowing through a resistor, R_a, connected between anode and H.T. supply produces sinusoidal variations in the anode voltage. The sign reversal between grid voltage and anode voltage is of importance.

The 'amplification factor μ', for the valve is defined as

$$\mu = \left(\frac{-dV_a}{dI_g}\right)_{I_a \text{const.}} \qquad 5.1(a)$$

For a typical triode μ may have a value between 20 and 80. For a pentode the value is somewhat larger. Two other ratios are important

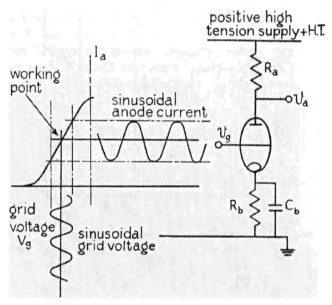

FIG. 5.3 Amplifying action of a triode stage

when considering the behaviour of valve stages. The 'mutual conductance g_m' relates anode current and grid voltage for constant anode voltage thus,

$$g_m = \left(\frac{dI_a}{dV_g}\right)_{V_a \text{const.}} \qquad 5.1(b)$$

Typical values for triodes and pentodes might lie between 1 mA/V, and 10 mA/V. The 'slope resistance r_a' for a valve is given by

$$r_a = \left(\frac{dV_a}{dI_a}\right)_{V_g \text{const.}} \qquad 5.1(c)$$

66 · ELECTRONIC ANALOGUE COMPUTERS

r_a might be of the order of 20 kΩ for a triode. For a pentode r_a might lie between 500 kΩ and 2 MΩ. The typical values quoted for μ, g_m, and r_a are intended to serve as a guide. They relate to linear regions of the valve characteristics. A batch of valves, nominally identical, might exhibit a variation of ± 20 per cent in the value of the parameters.

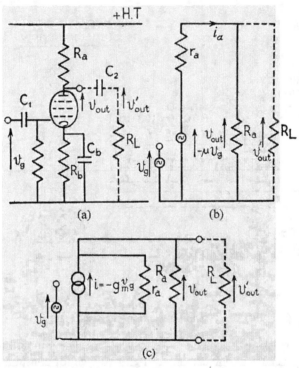

FIG. 5.4. Valve equivalent circuits. (a) Circuit diagram. (b) Constant voltage equivalent circuit. (c) Constant current equivalent circuit

A valve amplifying stage, provided that it is operated over its linear regime, may be represented by either a constant voltage or a constant current equivalent circuit. In either case the representation is restricted to signal quantities. The constant voltage equivalent circuit is used for triodes and pentodes. The constant current equivalent circuit is normally used only when considering pentode stages since as is seen from Fig. 5.2(c) the anode current is virtually constant over a wide range of operating conditions.

Figure 5.4(a) shows a simplified circuit diagram for a pentode amplifying stage. As with the triode already considered, resistor R_b and capacitor C_b constitute the bias circuit to ensure that the working point is such that operation is linear. Capacitor C_1 ensures that only a.c. signals are impressed upon the grid from the preceding stage. Similarly capacitor C_2 prevents d.c. signals from reaching the load resistor R_L connected between anode and earth.

Figure 5.4(b) is the constant voltage equivalent circuit for the pentode stage. It would be equally valid for a triode stage. Bias arrangements and coupling capacitors are omitted, since all capacitors are assumed to have negligible reactance at operating frequencies. In Fig. 5.4(b) the sign reversal of the signal is denoted by the use of the minus sign in the term $-\mu v_g$ at the voltage generator. From the equivalent circuit,

$$v_{\text{out}} = -\frac{\mu v_g R_a}{r_a + R_a} \qquad 5.2(a)$$

If the load resistor R_L is included, then

$$v'_{\text{out}} = -\frac{\mu v_g R}{r_a + R} \qquad 5.2(b)$$

where R is the parallel combination of R_a and R_L.

Figure 5.4(c) shows the constant current generator form of the equivalent circuit for a pentode valve stage. The output voltage v_{out} is given by,

$$v_{\text{out}} = -\frac{g_m v_g r_a R_a}{r_a + R_a} \qquad 5.3(a)$$

and if a load resistor R_L is included,

$$v'_{\text{out}} = -\frac{g_m v_g r_a R}{r_a + R} \qquad 5.3(b)$$

where R is the parallel combination of R_a and R_L.

A number of amplifying stages of the type shown in Fig. 5.4(a) may be connected in tandem to increase the overall gain of a complete amplifier. The essential features of such an amplifier are shown in

Fig. 5.5. V_1, V_2, and V_3 are triode valves providing voltage gain. Interstage resistance–capacitance coupling is provided by the capacitors C_2 and resistors R_g. A phase-shift of 180° occurs in each stage. The final stage is a 'cathode-follower'. The anode V_4 is connected directly to the positive H.T. supply. The output is taken across a resistor R_k connected between cathode and earth. The voltage

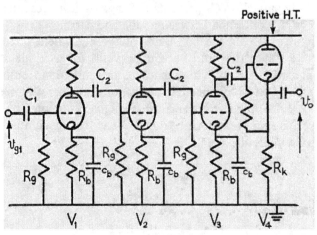

FIG. 5.5. Essential features of multi-stage amplifier

equivalent circuit of such a stage is shown in Fig. 5.6. Analysis of the circuit yields the following important results.

(i) The input impedance† Z_{in} is very large.

(ii) The output impedance† Z_{out} has a low value. Z_{out} is given by the following approximate relation

$$Z_{out} \simeq \frac{1}{g_m} \, \Omega \qquad\qquad 5.4$$

This impedance is shunted by the cathode resistor R_k.

† *Input impedance and output impedance.* Any active linear two-terminal network may be replaced by an equivalent circuit consisting of a voltage generator in series with an impedance (Thèvenin's Theorem). This impedance may be regarded as the input impedance Z_{in} when considering the input terminals of a network, or as the output impedance Z_{ou} when considering the output terminals.

(iii) The cathode-follower stage has approximately unity gain without phase reversal.

(iv) As a result of (i), (ii) and (iii) above, the cathode-follower provides current gain rather than voltage gain.

(v) The cathode resistor R_k provides a large amount of negative feedback with the result that changes in cathode potential follow changes in grid potential very closely. (Hence the name 'cathode follower').

A cathode-follower stage is frequently employed as the final stage

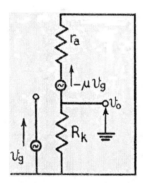

FIG. 5.6. Voltage equivalent circuit
of cathode follower

of a multi-stage amplifier. It is capable of delivering currents of the order of tens of milliamps from its low output impedance.

In the brief treatment above, the amplifying action of valve stages was considered in terms of a.c. signals for convenience. The reader is referred to any of the well-known texts on elementary electronics, Ref. 5.3 or 5.4, for example, for a fuller treatment.

As was pointed out in Chapter 3, however, amplifiers used for computing purposes must be capable of amplifying signals down to zero frequency, i.e. the amplifier must be capable of passing d.c. signals. This implies direct coupling between stages. Hence the term direct-coupled, or d.c., amplifier. Methods of attaining interstage coupling for d.c. signals are considered in the next section.

5.3 Features special to d.c. amplifiers

In the amplifier shown in Fig. 5.5 the capacitors C_2 isolate the d.c. components of the anode voltages from the grids of the succeeding valves. Thus so far as a.c. signals are concerned the grids of each valve

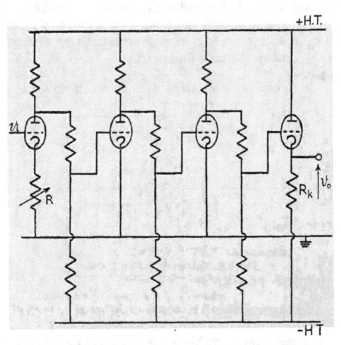

FIG. 5.7. Essential features of multi-stage d.c. amplifier

are at zero potential and the output is zero for zero input. For the direct-coupled amplifier however, the capacitors cannot be used. If the capacitors were merely omitted from the circuit the steady d.c. anode potential of one valve would appear at the grid of the next valve with the result that for satisfactory operation the valves would have to operate at successively higher electrode potentials. The output would have a large positive value even in the absence of an input signal.

To overcome these difficulties, interstage coupling is achieved through resistor chains such as those of Fig. 5.7 where a d.c. amplifier consisting of three amplifying stages with cathode-follower output is shown. The values of resistors are chosen such that under quiescent conditions, the potential at the output is approximately zero for zero input voltage. Both positive and negative signals may be handled. Such an arrangement necessitates a negative H.T. supply. The use of the resistor chains involves a loss of gain/stage compared with the corresponding a.c. amplifier. If the resistors of a chain from anode to the negative H.T. rail were equal, for example, then for a 10 mV swing at the anode say, only 5 mV would appear at the grid of the next stage. In the simple circuit shown, resistor R may be adjusted to ensure that the output is initially zero when the input voltage is zero. This is the process known as 'zero setting', ('Z.S.'), discussed in Chapter 4. In more elaborate amplifiers, zero setting is achieved rather differently.

In any event, however carefully the zero setting is performed, the output cannot be expected to remain zero indefinitely even though the input is at zero potential or is earthed. This output 'drift' is one of the principal problems associated with d.c. amplifiers. It may arise in one or more of the ways described in the next section.

5.4 Drift in d.c. amplifiers

(i) *Drift due to variation of H.T. supply voltages.* With an a.c. amplifier, small changes in H.T. potentials are unimportant. Changes in H.T. potential are important for d.c. amplifiers however. Consider the simple d.c. amplifier shown in Fig. 5.7 for example. A change in positive H.T. potential will result in a shift in anode potential of the first valve which will be transmitted via the potential chain to the grid of the next valve as a drift signal. Since this signal will be amplified in the second and third stages, drift at the first stage of an amplifier is more serious than that which occurs in subsequent stages. A change in negative H.T. potential will affect the three stages in a similar manner though, as before, drift at the first stage will be the most serious. Since the first stage of a d.c. amplifier is all important, special designs intended to minimize drift are frequently employed. These will be considered later.

In any event drift due to variation of H.T. supply voltages is minimized by the use of stabilized power supplies. Highly stabilized power supplies are readily available. The figures below are typical of a power supply of moderate performance.

Current range	0–1A
Voltage range	250–300 V
Output impedance at d.c.	0·2Ω
Output impedance up to 100 kc/s	0·5Ω
Stability factor for mains variation up to ± 10 per cent	200:1
Ripple and noise at output	500 mV.

A power supply with the above performance would be widely used in computing applications for all but the moxt exacting requirements. The good stability makes the output voltage insensitive to a.c. mains variations. The low output impedance provides good regulation. In addition the low output impedance ensures that coupling between the various stages of individual amplifiers and the computing elements of a complete machine, through the common power supply, is reduced to an absolute minimum.

Sometimes a power supply of even better performance is necessary. Such a power supply may be used to provide reference voltages of the order of ± 100V for such purposes as the initial conditions to be applied at integrators. For such applications it is frequently important to be able to set the positive and negative voltages equal and opposite as precisely as possible. Alternatively a power supply of the highest performance may be required for a computer when extreme accuracy of computation is needed. Typical figures for such a power supply are given below.

Current range	0–200 mA
Voltage output	± 100 V within 0·1 per cent long term (comparison against a Weston Standard Cell). Positive and negative voltages equal and opposite to within 5 mV long term
Stability factor	4000:1
d.c. output impedance	0·005Ω
Ripple and noise	less than 0·01 per cent.

Stabilized power supplied are discussed at length in Ref. 5.5.

(ii) *Drift due to changes in heater voltage.* The effect of a change in heater voltage is to alter the cathode temperature and hence the initial velocity with which electrons are emitted from the cathode. (The subject of thermionic emission is discussed very fully in texts dealing with the physics of thermionic emission, for example, Ref. 5.6). As a result the grid potential required for a constant anode current will change. The effect of the change of heater voltage may therefore be expressed in terms of the amount by which the cathode voltage must be changed with respect to the grid voltage in order that the anode current remains constant. A figure of 0·2 V for a 20 per cent change of heater voltage is quoted by the author of Ref. 5.7. This implies that a change of 20 per cent in heater voltage will have the same effect as a signal of 0·2 V applied to the grid of a valve stage. This will be particularly important at the first stage of an amplifier.

The techniques to be discussed in connection with Section (i) above offer some compensation against the effects of change in heater voltage. In addition some degree of stabilization of heater voltage may be considered desirable. Since heater supplies are usually a.c., a 'constant voltage' transformer can be connected between the a.c. mains supply and the heater transformer. In this way a substantial improvement in the stability of the heater voltage can be attained. With earlier types the waveform would be far from sinusoidal. Constant voltage transformers which provide a sinusoidal output are now available. Typical performance figures for small transformers of this type are given below.

Rating	1000 VA
Stability factor	400:1 for input variations of ± 10 per cent at full load
Output impedance	15Ω
Harmonic distortion	less than 3 per cent on full load
	less than 5 per cent on no load

(iii) *Drift due to changes in resistance values.* Changes in the resistance values of the resistors in a d.c. amplifier can produce drift signals. Small changes in the values of the resistors of the interstage chain of Fig. 5.7, for example, will result in spurious voltages at the grids of subsequent stages. These effects may be minimized by the use of

6

high-stability resistors operated well within their wattage rating to minimize resistance changes due to heating.

Great care should be taken to keep the temperature of the computing amplifiers as low as possible and to avoid local overheating due to poor mechanical design. The same applies to the complete machine. While adequate ventilation and temperature control of the computing room is desirable, and indeed essential for accurate work, Shaw (Ref. 5.8) has shown that much can be achieved by careful attention to the design of amplifier chasses, panel layouts, and cabinets.

(iv) *Drift due to changes in valve characteristics.* The performance of valves varies with time. The values of μ, r_a, and g_m change. Cathode emission falls off comparatively rapidly during the first few hundred hours operation, and then more slowly. This produces results similar to those caused by heater voltage variations. Occasionally even complete failure may occur during initial operation. After this initial period performance settles down.

Valves may be 'aged' by running them under conditions similar to operating conditions for some hundreds of hours before use in the computer. On occasion such a procedure may be deemed desirable, especially in a large installation. Considerable work on the performance of valves in continuous use has been done, see, for example, Ref. 5.9.

(v) *Drift due to grid current.* In the preliminary statement of criteria for a successful computing amplifier, negligible grid current was assumed. In practice small grid currents are present even when a valve is operated in normal fashion with negative grid bias (Ref. 5.7 and 5.10). This grid current comprises two components.

(*a*) *Negative grid current.* Positive ions which are produced as a result of the ionization of residual gases in the valve are attracted to the negative grid. This flow constitutes a conventional current flowing out at the grid terminal.

(*b*) *Positive grid current.* This occurs due to the arrival at the grid wires of thermal electrons which are sufficiently energetic to overcome the negative potential gradient.

For a particular value of negative grid potential the two components of grid current are equal and opposite. For other values the current will be either positive or negative. Typical grid current values with valves used in computers will be of the order of 10^{-9} to 10^{-11} A. Such grid currents provide a further source of drift voltage particularly serious in integrators.

Consider the diagram shown in Fig. 5.8. The input resistor R_i is earthed at the end remote from the grid of the first stage of the computing amplifier. This ensures zero input signal v_i.

Suppose that a grid current i_g flows out of the first stage, and as a result the potential of the grid changes by δv_g from the zero potential

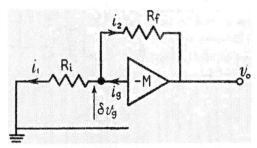

FIG. 5.8. Drift due to grid current

of the virtual earth condition. Currents i_1 and i_2 flow in the input resistor R_i and the feedback resistor R_f respectively. Now

$$i_1 = \frac{\delta v_g}{R_i} \quad \text{and} \quad i_2 = \frac{\delta v_g - v_o}{R_f}$$

where v_o is the output voltage resulting from the grid current, Also

$$v_o = \delta v_g(-M) \quad \text{hence} \quad i_2 = \frac{\delta v_g(1+M)}{R_f}$$

Comparison of i_1 and i_2 shows that for normal values of R_i and R_f, $i_g \simeq i_2$. Hence the grid current may be considered as flowing almost entirely into R_f to produce the output drift voltage $v_o \simeq i_g R_f$. The process of 'zero setting' will reduce this to zero. Unfortunately the value of grid current will not remain constant, but will change during valve operation. Sometimes it may be possible to choose a valve with low grid current for the first stage of an amplifier. Alternatively operation with low anode voltage reduces grid current.

Importance of first stage. The importance of the first stage as a source of drift has already been mentioned. It is useful to consider the analysis of a multistage amplifier with feedback to emphasize the need to reduce drift in input stages to the absolute minimum.

Consider the three-stage amplifier shown in Fig. 5.9. v is the input voltage and v_o the output voltage, a fraction of which, β, is fed back

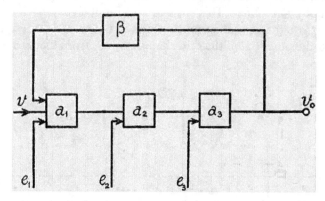

FIG. 5.9. Block diagram of multi-stage amplifier with drift voltages e_1, e_2 and e_3

to the input of the first stage. β is frequently called the 'feedback ratio'. The gains of the individual stages are a_1, a_2, and a_3 respectively, where a_1, a_2, and a_3 are negative quantities. The overall gain is the product $a_1 a_2 a_3$. At the grids of the three stages drift voltages e_1, e_2, and e_3 appear due to the effects discussed in the earlier part of the section.

The output voltage, v_o, is given by,

$$v_o = v(a_1 a_2 a_3) + e_1(a_1 a_2 a_3) + e_2(a_2 a_3) + \beta\{v_o(a_1 a_2 a_3)\}$$

Rearrangement gives,

$$v_o = \frac{v(a_1 a_2 a_3) + e_1(a_1 a_2 a_3) + e_2(a_2 a_3) + e_3 a_3}{1 - \beta a_1 a_2 a_3} \qquad 5.5$$

Consider the case where the output is not zero due to the presence of the drift voltages e_1, e_2, and e_3. Regard the input voltage v as a voltage applied at the first stage with the object of restoring the output voltage, v_o, to zero. Then v_o will be zero if the numerator of eqn. 5.5 is set equal to zero, i.e. if,

$$v(a_1 a_2 a_3) = -\{e_1(a_1 a_2 a_3) + e_2(a_2 a_3) + e_3 a_3\}$$

or

$$v = -\left\{e_1 + \frac{1}{a_1} e_2 + \frac{1}{a_1 a_2} . e_3\right\} \qquad 5.6$$

This voltage v required at the input grid of an amplifier to restore the output voltage to zero in the presence of drift, is equal in magnitude and opposite in sign to the 'drift voltage referred to input'. The performance of a computing amplifier with regard to drift is usually discussed in terms of this quantity.

Consideration of eqn. 5.6 in the light of some typical values is of considerable interest. Suppose $a_1 = a_2 = a_3 = -20$, and

$$e_1 = e_2 = e_3 = 10 \, \text{mV}$$

Then

$$v = -\left\{1 - \frac{1}{20} + \frac{1}{20^2}\right\} 10 \times 10^{-3} \, \text{volts}$$

This clearly shows that the value of the drift referred to input depends almost entirely on the drift in the first stage. The design of input stages with a view to minimizing drift will be considered in the next section.

Consider next the computing amplifier shown in Fig. 5.10(a) with input resistor R_i and feedback resistor R_f having the input resistor earthed. Suppose that the output drift is considered to be due to drift, e_1, in the input stage only. The diagram has been rearranged in Fig. 5.10(b) to show that under these circumstances the feedback ratio β is given by,

$$\beta = \frac{R_i}{R_i + R_f} \qquad 5.7$$

For such an amplifier the output voltage v_o is given by,

$$v_o = e_1(-M) + \beta v_o(-M) \qquad 5.8$$

where $(-M)$ is the open-loop gain. The relation can be rewritten thus,

$$v_o = \frac{e_1(-M)}{1 - \dfrac{R_i}{R_i + R_f}(-M)} \qquad 5.9$$

Consider the typical case of an amplifier of moderate performance with $R_i = R_f$, and $M = 10,000$. Then $v_o \simeq 2e_1$ represents an excellent

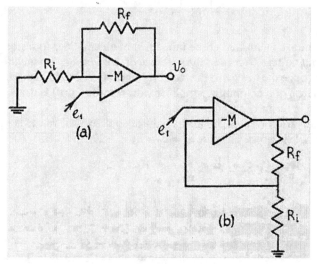

FIG. 5.10. Two aspects of a computing amplifier

approximation. For a typical value of output drift voltage $v_o = 25\,\mathrm{mV}$, the drift referred to input, e_1, would be $12 \cdot 5\,\mathrm{mV}$.

Evaluation of drift in a computing amplifier under test sometimes involves the measurement of inconveniently small voltages. The above example serves to illustrate one possible technique which minimizes the difficulty. The computing amplifier is set up with a ratio of feedback to input resistor of say,

$$\frac{R_f}{R_i} = \frac{9}{1}$$

Then the feedback ratio, β, is given by,

$$\beta = \frac{R_i}{R_i + R_f} = \frac{1}{10}$$

Equation 5.9 yields $e_1 = 0.1\, v_o$. Thus the drift referred to input is one tenth that measured on a voltmeter at the output of the amplifier. For the example above, the quantity to be measured would become 125 mV.

Drift has a serious effect on the performance of integrators. Usually a drift voltage has a bias towards either negative or positive values. In such cases the operational amplifier will integrate the drift voltage with respect to time. The continual increase in output voltage due to this cause sets a limit to the total computing time. Observation of the output of an operational amplifier connected as an integrator, and having the input resistor earthed, is an excellent guide to drift performance.

5.5 Input stages for d.c. amplifiers

It was shown in the last section that to minimize the drift at the input stage of a d.c. amplifier was most important. Various circuits have been devised to this end and are described in the literature (Ref. 5.7 and 5.10). Circuits based on the 'long-tail pair' arrangement are frequently used for this purpose. The elements of such a circuit are shown in Fig. 5.11. The behaviour is described qualitatively below.

V_1 and V_2 may be the halves of a double triode. Alternatively they may be a pair of matched valves. The common cathode connection is taken through a large resistance R_k to the negative H.T. rail. Let V_k be the volt-drop across the cathode resistor in the absence of input signals to either grid. The current, I_k, through R_f will be given by,

$$I_k = \frac{V_k}{R_k}$$

Three methods of operation are possible depending on the manner in which signals are applied to the grids of the valves.

(i) *Common-anode operation:* $v_1 = v_2 = v$ *volts.* Because of the heavy negative feedback provided by the cathode-follower action due to the presence of resistor R_k, the cathode potential will be near the grid potentials. Now suppose that small positive signal voltages v_1 and v_2 of equal magnitude v volts are applied to the grids. The cathode voltage will rise by about v volts. Since $v \ll V_k$, the new value of the volt-drop across the cathode resistor, V_k' say, will not be very different from V_k. Hence the modified value of the cathode current I_k', will not be significantly different from I_k. Indeed the cathode current

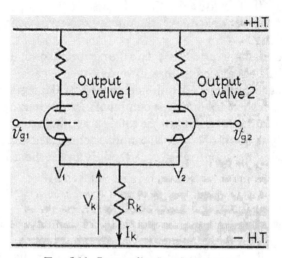

FIG. 5.11. Long-tail pair using triodes

may be regarded as a constant. Suppose, for example, that due to signals v_1 and v_2 the cathode potential has shifted through 1·0 V. Then for typical values, $R_k = 33$ kΩ and $V_k = 200$ V,

$$I_k = \frac{V_k}{R_k} = \frac{200}{33} \text{ mA} = 6\cdot06 \text{ mA}$$

and
$$I_k' = \frac{V_k'}{R_k} = \frac{201}{33} \text{ mA} = 6\cdot10 \text{ mA}$$

Since the cathode current is a constant, the anode currents are constant. An output appears at neither anode. Even more accurately the difference between the anode voltages is also zero. The differential output between the anodes is also zero.

(ii) *Push-pull operation:* $v_1 = v$ *volts,* $v_2 = -v$ *volts.* When equal and opposite signals are applied to the grids, the anode current of one valve increases, and that of the other decreases by an equal amount. The cathode potential is unchanged. Under these conditions negative feedback no longer applies. Each valve amplifies separately. The gain of each is given by eqn. 5.2 for triode valves or eqn. 5.3 for pentodes. The potential at the anode of V_1, falls by δV_a and that at V_2 rises by δV_a. Again a matched pair is assumed.

(iii) *Single-ended operation:* $v_1 = v$ *volts,* $v_2 = 0$ *volts.* The behaviour of a matched pair in this case is best discussed in two sections. First take $+\frac{1}{2}v$ volts applied to both V_1 and V_2. As was seen in Section (i) above this has negligible effect. Next apply $+\frac{1}{2}v$ to valve V_1 and $-\frac{1}{2}v$ to valve V_2. Signals $-\frac{1}{2}\delta V_a$ and $+\frac{1}{2}\delta V_a$ appear as described in Section (ii). The overall effect is that which would occur if v volts were applied to V_1 only. The difference, or push-pull, output which appears across the two anodes is

$$2 \times \frac{\delta V_a}{2} = \delta V_a$$

This push-pull output is equal to the gain of a normal single stage.

The analysis of the long-tail pair circuit is discussed in detail in Ref. 5.10.

The value of the long-tail pair circuit is apparent when the above cases are considered. Take first the common-mode operation of Section (i). Any drift common to both valves will be equivalent to signals of the common-mode type. Drift due to variation of H.T. supply voltage is largely of this type (5.4 (i)). So too is drift due to changes in heater voltage (5.4.(ii)). Improvement in drift performance is especially marked if the valves are matched. Drift due to changes in valve characteristics (5.4. (iv)) is also reduced by the use of the long-tail pair circuit.

The long-tail pair circuit may be used as an input stage in one of two ways.

(*a*) *Single-ended operation.* In this case the input signal is applied to one grid, the other is either earthed, or connected to a potential-divider chain suitable for Z.S. adjustment. Output voltages are taken at the anodes of the valves. The differential output is about equal to that of a normal single stage. Such a circuit for pentode valves is shown in Fig. 5.12.

(*b*) *Push-pull operation.* In some cases drift is minimized by the use of an auxiliary amplifier which precedes the main amplifier. This

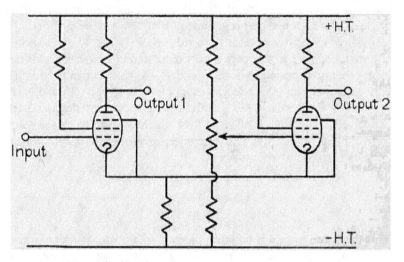

FIG. 5.12 Single-ended operation of long-tail pair

subject will be dealt with in a later section. When such an amplifier is used, it may be convenient to apply the input signal to one grid, and a signal which has passed through the auxiliary amplifier to the other. This is push-pull operation. Such a circuit is shown in Fig. 5.13. The potentiometer R is adjusted initially to ensure zero output in the absence of signal input.

In some cases the outputs of the long-tail pair circuits discussed above are taken to a second push-pull stage, before further amplification. A cathode-follower output stage would probably be added for the reasons mentioned in Section 5.2.

Alternatively the output at only one anode of the long-tail pair might be used, and the remainder of the amplifier consist of single valve stages, with a final cathode-follower stage.

The question of overall gain is an important one. High gain, open loop, is desirable for most computing amplifier applications. Unfortunately the attainment of high gain poses serious stability problems. Without considerable care in the amplifier design, positive feedback with sustained oscillations in the absence of signals will occur. For

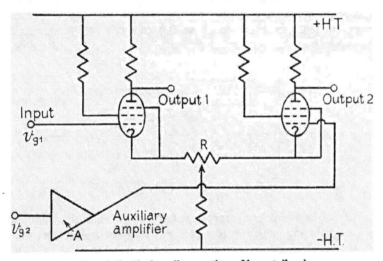

FIG. 5.13. Push-pull operation of long-tail pair

this reason d.c. amplifiers of the type discussed above will normally have no more than three, or possibly five, stages of gain.

A discussion of amplifier design with reference to stability is beyond the scope of this book. The reader is referred to the texts on feedback amplifier design (Refs. 5.11 and 5.12).

5.6 Use of an auxiliary amplifier to obviate drift

Although circuits of the long-tail pair type result in enhanced drift performance some drift remains. Periodic balancing of the amplifier is still necessary. The need for computing amplifiers which could be considered virtually drift-free led to more sophisticated designs in

which an additional auxiliary amplifier is used in association with a
d.c. amplifier of the type described above. Such methods are considered in Refs. 5.13 and 5.14 among others. Although the technique is
often described as 'drift correction', and the overall amplifier as a
'drift-corrected' amplifier, the analysis below indicates that these
terms may be rather misleading. The term 'chopper-stabilization'
also is used on occasion. The reason for this will become apparent
later in the section. With such drift-corrected amplifiers continuous
operation over a period of hours, or even days, is frequently possible.

The importance of drift at the first stage of a computing amplifier
was emphasized in the analysis of Section 5.4. Consider now the

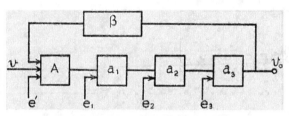

FIG. 5.14. Use of auxiliary amplifier

effect of an additional amplifier of gain A added to the front end of
the main amplifier. Figure 5.14 shows the circuit. As before v is the
input voltage and v_o the output voltage, a fraction of which, β, is fed
back to the input of the first stage. Drift signals e', e_1, e_2, and e_3 appear
at the input to the stages. The output voltage v_o is given by,

$$v_o = v(Aa_1 a_2 a_3) + e'(Aa_1 a_2 a_3) + e_1(a_1 a_2 a_3) +$$
$$e_2(a_2 a_3) + e_3(a_3) + \beta\{v_o(Aa_1 a_2 a_3)\}$$

Rearrangement yields,

$$v_o = \frac{v(Aa_1 a_2 a_3) + e'(Aa_1 a_2 a_3) + e_1(a_1 a_2 a_3) + e_2(a_2 a_3) + e_3(a_3)}{1 - \beta Aa_1 a_2 a_3}$$

5.10

Take the case where the output, v_o is not zero due to the drift
voltages e', e_1, e_2, and e_3. Consider that the input voltages v is applied

at the first stage with the object of restoring the output voltage, v_o, to zero. v_o will be zero if the numerator of eqn. 5.10 is set equal to zero, i.e. if,

$$v = -\left\{ e' + \frac{e_1}{A} + \frac{e_2}{Aa_1} + \frac{e_3}{Aa_1 a_2} \right\} \qquad 5.11$$

As before v is equal in magnitude, and opposite in sign, to the drift voltage with respect to input. Equation 5.11 shows that the principal contribution to drift arises from the drift voltage, e', just as previously eqn. 5.6 indicated that the voltage e_1 was the main contribution. Thus for the previous case, with zero input voltage v, approximation of eqn. 5.5 yields,

$$v_o \simeq \frac{a_1 a_2 a_3}{1 - \beta a_1 a_2 a_3} . e_1 \text{ but } \beta a_1 a_2 a_3 \gg 1$$

hence
$$v_o \simeq \frac{-a_1 a_2 a_3}{\beta a_1 a_2 a_3} . e_1 = -\frac{e_1}{\beta} \qquad 5.12$$

Now consider what happens when the additional amplifier is inserted, and the input voltage is again assumed to be zero. Taking the first two terms, an approximation of eqn. 5.10 gives.

$$v_o \simeq \frac{e'(Aa_1 a_2 a_3) + e_1(a_1 a_2 a_3)}{1 - \beta Aa_1 a_2 a_3} \text{ but } \beta Aa_1 a_2 a_3 \gg 1$$

hence
$$v_o \simeq -\left\{ \frac{e'}{\beta} + \frac{e_1}{\beta A} \right\} \qquad 5.12(a)$$

Now suppose that a convenient method existed by which the drift voltage, e', could be made very small. If the gain A had a value of say 500, then the output voltage, v_o, due to drift would be simply,

$$v_o \simeq -\left\{ \frac{e_1}{\beta A} \right\} \qquad 5.12(b)$$

The drift performance would thus be improved by a factor of A times.

Drift in the auxiliary amplifier is avoided by arranging that it is a.c. coupled. The small d.c. or low frequency input signal is converted to

an a.c. signal by the action of a mechanical modulator which provides
at the input of the auxiliary amplifier a rectangular wave, the amplitude of which is proportional to the d.c. signal applied. Phase sensitive
demodulation follows amplification in the a.c. amplifier. In practice
a single electromechanical relay is used to perform both functions.
It is vibrated by the application of an alternating current of convenient
frequency. Typical operating frequencies range from 50 c/s to 400 c/s.

A block diagram showing the relay operation is given in Fig. 5.15.
A resistor R_a is connected between the summing point and the input
to the auxiliary amplifier. With the relay as shown in position 1 the

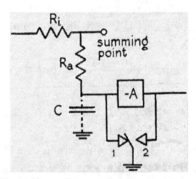

FIG. 5.15. Relay used for modulation and demodulation

input to the auxiliary amplifier is earthed. No signal appears at the
grid of the first stage. At the same time a signal can be taken from the
output. When the relay moves to position 2 a potential similar to that
at the summing point appears at the grid and the output is clamped
to earth potential. The diagrams of Fig. 5.16 illustrate the operation
of the auxiliary amplifier under the action of the relay. The waveform
at the summing point is shown at (a). The position of the relay contact
during equal time intervals is shown at (b). The chopped waveform
at the input to the auxiliary amplifier which results from the action
of the relay is given at (c). Amplification of the a.c. component shown
at (d), follows. The amplified wave is shown at (e). The waveform
which results from the action of the chopper on the output signal is
shown at (f). It will be noticed that due to the action of the chopper

relay this output waveform is of the opposite sign to the input wave. As will be seen later in the section, this sign reversal is often convenient in practical designs where auxiliary amplifiers are employed. In any event there must be a sign reversal in the amplifier considered as a

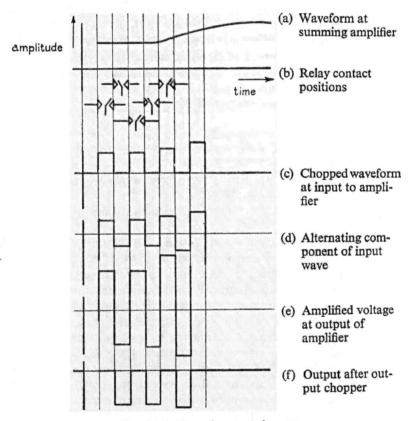

amplitude

time

(a) Waveform at summing amplifier

(b) Relay contact positions

(c) Chopped waveform at input to amplifier

(d) Alternating component of input wave

(e) Amplified voltage at output of amplifier

(f) Output after output chopper

FIG. 5.16. Wave forms at chopper

whole. The above waveforms are shown in an idealized way. In practice they will be far from rectangular due to the effects of attenuation of the higher frequency components in the amplifier, switching transients, contact bounce, relay noise, etc.

In early designs relay performance proved a serious limitation to the use of auxiliary amplifiers. The life of such relays was restricted to some hundreds of hours. With more recent relays performance has been improved and life considerably extended.

The output wave is smoothed using a suitable filter circuit. It is the attenuation characteristic of the filter circuit which is chiefly responsible for the restricted bandwidth of the auxiliary amplifier. Typical values might be between 2 c/s and 5 c/s.

In some cases a capacitor C is included at the input to the auxiliary amplifier. The combination of R_a and C constitutes a low-pass filter, restricting higher frequency signals to the main d.c. amplifier. Capacitor C also provides a measure of drift correction by virtue of integral-control negative feedback. A drift signal at the summing

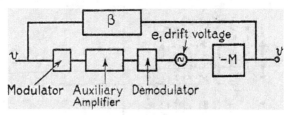

FIG. 5.17. Amplifiers in series

point will produce an output signal of the opposite sign. Under these circumstances a current will flow through the feedback resistor which will charge capacitor C in a sense such as to cancel the original drift signal. A measure of correction will remain as the capacitor discharges.

In practice it is normally considered undesirable to connect the auxiliary and main amplifiers in series as shown in Fig. 5.17 and implied by the block diagram of Fig. 5.14. For the series connection of Fig. 5.17 the overall gain is given by the product of the two gains $A \times M$. As a result the overall bandwidth is restricted to that of the a.c. amplifier. This is unsatisfactory for many computing applications. Figure 5.18 shows a rather different arrangement.

The input signal, v, is applied to the main amplifier directly and also via the auxiliary amplifier. This corresponds to a slight modification of eqn. 5.10 to give $v\{(A+1)a_1 a_2 a_3\}$ as the first term on the right-hand side rather than $v(Aa_1 a_2 a_3)$. Since A has typically a value of some hundreds at d.c., eqn. 5.12 is still valid.

The manner in which the two signals fed to the main amplifier are combined has not been specified. One convenient way is to apply them as difference signals to the two grids of a long-tail pair. Under these conditions a sign reversal is required in the auxiliary amplifier. This is the arrangement shown in Fig. 5.13.

At d.c. $Av \gg v$ and operation will approximate to single-ended working with overall gain equal to the product $A \times M$. For some frequency of comparatively low value, say 5 c/s, $Av \simeq v$ and operation will be push-pull, while at higher frequencies operation will again be single ended with overall gain M. No matter how low the gain of the auxiliary amplifier falls, the overall gain will never be less than M.

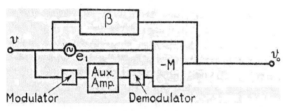

FIG. 5.18. Practical amplifier connection

In the above treatment on the use of an auxiliary amplifier to minimize drift, the emphasis has been on the concept of the importance of a 'drift-free' first stage as applied to the analysis leading to eqn. 5.12. This method clearly indicates the value of the auxiliary amplifier with its drift-free gain. In addition increased gain $A \times M$ at d.c. and low frequencies provides the other advantages which follow from high open-loop gain.

For this reason little stress has been placed on the other aspect of drift minimization whereby the auxiliary amplifier is seen as providing a 'drift-correction' signal directly by the application of a correcting signal at one grid of a long-tail pair when a drift signal of small amplitude occurs at the other.

It is sometimes convenient to provide a neon lamp across the output terminals of the auxiliary amplifier. Under conditions of serious departure of the summing point from zero potential, a large output will occur at the auxiliary amplifier. Such a departure may occur as a

7

drift voltage due to some malfunctioning of either amplifier. Alternatively it may be due to an excessively large signal applied to the computing amplifier which results in overload of the final stage. The warning neon will be illuminated in either event.

5.7 Performance of valve computing amplifiers

Before leaving the subject of valve computing amplifiers it is instructive to consider the development in performance which has resulted since their introduction.

One of the first references to the use of electronic analogue computers is the paper by Ragazzini, Randall, and Russell (Ref. 5.15) published in 1947. The d.c. amplifier used in their work had a gain of about 5000. As a precaution against drift the input stage consisted of a long-tail pair circuit in which the halves of a double triode were used. The second and third stages also consisted of the halves of a double triode. Conventional production valves were used. The H.T. supplies were ± 350 volts and -190 volts. Chopper stabilization was not used. The complete computer was quite small and was mounted on two or three tables in a laboratory. The authors describe the use of the machine in the solution of problems concerning second-order mechanical systems and the motion of an aircraft in the pitch plane.

A much larger machine is discussed by Spearman, Gait, Hemingway, and Hynes (Ref. 5.16). Their paper describes the construction and operation of TRIDAC which was built at the Royal Aircraft Establishment between 1950 and 1954. TRIDAC is a machine suitable for the calculation in three dimensions of the trajectories of two aircraft or missiles with respect to each other. Since the machine contains several hundred computing amplifiers it was necessary to ensure that performance, especially as to drift, was good. The amplifiers were therefore of the drift-corrected type. The main d.c. amplifier had three stages of gain with cathode-follower output resulting in a gain of 60,000. The first stage was a long-tail pair. The input valve was of a type with low grid current and was operated with low anode potential to reduce the grid current further. As a result grid currents of the order of 10^{-11} A were achieved. The H.T. supplies were ± 300 V and ± 170 V. The swing for linear operation was ± 30 V. The auxiliary amplifier comprised two stages of gain with cathode-follower output.

This amplifier had a gain of about 1000. The chopping relay vibrated at 400 c/s. The drift at the output with unity gain was less than 1 mV.

Some typical performance figures for the more modern types of valve computing amplifier are given by Korn and Korn (Ref. 5.1). They are detailed below:

Gain of d.c. amplifier	30,000 to 150,000
Gain of auxiliary amplifier	2000 to 3000
Overall gain	25×10^6 to 300×10^6
r.m.s. noise referred to input	2 to 10 mV.

Average drift over eight hours, referred to input 20 to 200 μV, linear output swing ± 100 V.

REFERENCES

5.1. KORN, A. G., and KORN, T. M. *Electronic Analog Computers*, McGraw-Hill, New York, 1956.

5.2. WASS, C. A. A. *An Introduction to Electronic Analogue Computers*, Pergamon Press. London, 1956.

5.3. WILLIAMS, E. *Thermionic Valve Circuits*, Pitman, London, 1955.

5.4. AGGER, L. T. *Principles of Electronics*, Macmillan, London, 1956.

5.5. BENSON, F. A. *Voltage Stabilized Supplies: Basic Principles, Characteristics and Applications*, Macdonald, London, 1957.

5.6. PARKER, P. *Electronics*, Ch. VI, Edward Arnold, London, 1952.

5.7. VALLEY, G., and WALLMAN, R. (eds.) *Vacuum Tube Amplifiers*, Ch. II, McGraw-Hill, New York, 1948.

5.8. SHAW, E. N. 'Heat control in electronic equipment', *Electron. Engng*, **29**, Jan. p. 13, Feb. p. 65, Mar. p. 115, 1957.

5.9. BREWER, R. 'Radio valve testing', *Proc. I.E.E.*, **98**, Part III, 269, 1951.

5.10. GRAY, T. S. *Applied Electronics*, 2nd Ed. Ch. IX, John Wiley, New York, 1954.

5.11. NYQUIST, H. 'Regeneration theory', *Bell Syst. tech. J.*, **11**, No. 1, Jan. p. 126, 1932.

5.12 BODE, R. W. *Network Analysis and Feedback Amplifier Design*, Van Nostrand, New York, 1945.

5.13. GOLDBERG, E. A. 'Stabilization of d.c. amplifiers', *R.C.A. Review*, **2**, 296, 1950.

5.14. KANDIAH, K., and BROWN, D. E. 'High gain d.c. amplifiers', *Proc. I.E.E.*, **99**, Part II, 314, 1952.

5.15. RAGAZZINI, J. R., RANDALL, R. A., and RUSSELL, F. A. 'Analysis of problems in dynamics by electronic circuits', *Proc. I.R.E.*, **35**, 444, 1947.

5.16. SPEARMAN, F. R. J., GAIT, J. J., HEMINGWAY, A. V., and HYNES, R. W. 'Tridac, a large analogue computing machine', *Proc. I.E.E.*, **103**, B, 375, 1956.

CHAPTER 6

Transistor Computing Amplifiers

6.1 Introduction

In the last chapter the essential features of d.c. valve amplifiers used in computing were considered. Computing amplifiers using transistors rather than valves are now coming into operation. After a brief account of transistor action, some idea of the application of transistors to computing amplifiers will be given. Their performance will be compared with that of the conventional valve amplifiers.

6.2 Transistor action

The junction transistor has been developed over recent years to a state where it is a most valuable alternative to the thermionic valve for electronic applications. The mechanism of operation of a transistor is fundamentally more complicated than that of the triode or pentode valve. The reader is referred to the following texts, among many others, for details (Refs. 6.1, 6.2, and 6.3). The treatment below is intended only as a brief outline.

The material used in transistors are semiconductors of Group IV of the periodic table. Germanium (Ge) and silicon (Si) are the two commonly employed. In their normal state the conduction-band for their orbital electrons is empty. There are no vacancies in the valence-band. The four electrons in this band form covalent bonds with adjacent atoms. An electron excited to a conduction-band leaves behind an unoccupied valance-band state.

This deficiency has the properties of a positive charge carrier and is called a hole to distinguish it from the corresponding negative mobile charge carrier, the electron. Excitation of an electron to a conduction-band, with the consequent creation of a hole is thermal carrier generation. Thermally generated holes and electrons appear in equal numbers. Although it takes place at room temperature, a rise in temperature results in increased thermal carrier generation. A semiconductor which possesses conduction holes and electrons by virtue of thermal energy is an intrinsic semiconductor.

93

For transistor applications small quantities of impurities are added to the intrinsic semiconductor to provide an extrinsic semiconductor.

The introduction of a small amount of pentavalent impurity such as arsenic, phosphorus or antimony, only four of whose electrons take up covalent bonds leaves the fifth only loosely bound to the parent atom. This is readily available for conduction. The pentavalent impurity atom is called a donor. The semiconductor crystal is called n-type since it contains an excess of negative carriers. These are called majority carriers to distinguish them from the small number of positive carriers (holes) which are present due to thermal generation. These positive carriers are the minority carriers.

The introduction of a small amount of trivalent impurity such as gallium, indium or boron means that at intervals in the lattice of the crystal structure there is a deficiency of an electron in one of the covalent bonds. This lack constitutes a hole. Since electron transfer can take place in the covalent bonds, the hole is not restricted in its location. Indeed holes are available for conduction like the electrons of the donor type crystal. These are now the majority carriers while thermally generated electrons are minority carriers. Impurity atoms of the trivalent type are acceptor impurities. The semiconductor crystal is called p-type.

A piece of n-type semiconductor in contact with a piece of p-type constitutes a semiconductor junction diode. Current flow across the junction will consist of both holes and electrons. The magnitude of the current will depend on the polarity of a d.c. bias voltage applied across the junction and also on the temperature of the junction. Before the application of an external bias supply, the diffusion of holes of the p-type into the n-type region, and the diffusion of electrons of the n-type region into the p-type region leaves the p-type with a net negative charge and the n-type with a net positive charge. The electric field which appears in the vicinity of the junction inhibits further net carrier migration. An equilibrium condition is established with the flow of majority carriers due to diffusion balanced by the drift of minority carriers due to the presence of the electric field.

The graph of Fig. 6.1(b) shows the variation of current I with applied voltage V. The relation is seen to be non-linear. When reverse bias is applied the forward current falls to zero. The condition of reverse bias however is favourable to the flow of minority carriers. Thermally generated holes of the n region and electrons of the p region are swept easily across the boundary to constitute a saturation current I_s. This saturation current is substantially independent of the applied potential. Its magnitude is proportional to minority carrier density. Since these are thermally generated, the saturation current is proportional to temperature. It will be seen later that this current

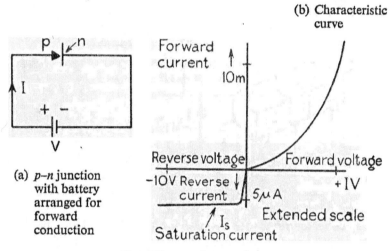

(b) Characteristic curve

(a) p–n junction with battery arranged for forward conduction

FIG. 6.1. p–n characteristics

provides one of the most important obstacles to successful operation of transistor d.c. amplifiers.

Figure 6.2(a) shows a schematic diagram of a junction transistor. It comprises three sections, emitter, base, and collector. Their functions may be compared very approximately to the cathode, grid, and anode of the thermionic triode. Some important differences will appear however. In Britain the emitter and collector are usually of p-type semiconductor material while the base is n-type. Bias arrangements for conventional operation are shown in Fig. 6.2(b). It will be seen that the emitter-base junction is biased for forward conduction, while the base-collector junction is biased for reverse conduction. Emitter and collector regions are heavily doped with p-type impurity.

The concentration of holes in these regions is greater than that of the concentration of electrons in the n-type base region.

Current flow through the base region consists mainly of holes from the emitter which pass by virtue of the forward bias applied to the emitter-base junction. Most sweep across to the collector where they flow out as collector current, I_c. Others recombine with electrons. The position is complicated by a variety of other factors such as dependence of the action on collector voltage, V_{cb}, the emitter-base voltage, V_{be}, and the presence of the saturation current, I_{co}, for the

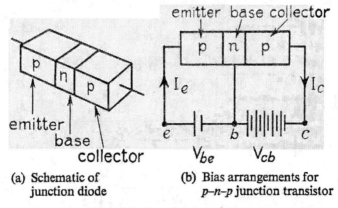

(a) Schematic of junction diode

(b) Bias arrangements for p–n–p junction transistor

FIG. 6.2. Junction transistor

base-collector diode which is reverse biased. The relation between net collector current, I_c, and net emitter current, I_e, is given by

$$\alpha_0 = \left(\frac{dI_c}{dI_e}\right)_{V_{cb}} \qquad\qquad 6.1$$

For junction transistors α_0 has a value which is a little less than unity. The relation between I_c and I_e may be far from linear for the above and other reasons. As with the thermionic valve, which was also seen to be a non-linear device, families of characteristic curves are valuable when considering transistor behaviour. If linear operation over restricted ranges of the characteristic curves is assumed, then equivalent circuits may be employed in the estimation of transistor circuit performance. For any particular set of operating conditions the following equations are valid for current flow in the diagram of Fig. 6.2(b).

Out of collector

$$I_c = \alpha_0 I_e + I_{co} \qquad\qquad 6.2(a)$$

Out of base

$$I_b = (I_e - \alpha_0 I_e) - I_{co}$$

or

$$I_b = (1 - \alpha_0) I_e - I_{co} \qquad\qquad 6.2(b)$$

Whereas the thermionic valve was seen to be essentially a voltage operated device, the transistor is a current device. This notion will become apparent as the characteristic curves are examined.

The transistor may be operated in one of three ways depending on which of the terminals is taken as common or grounded. Transistor circuit behaviour is determined by the configuration used.

6.3 Transistor equivalent circuits

(i) *Common or grounded base operation.* Figure 6.3(a) shows the common base arrangement which has the alternative name of grounded base. This is analogous to grounded grid valve operation though there are important differences. The base terminal is common to input and output circuits. An input current flowing in at the emitter terminal provides an output current flowing out at the collector. Alternatively a voltage input applied between emitter and base provides a corresponding voltage output developed across a load resistor connected between collector and base. Bias arrangements are shown using batteries, but in practice more convenient methods are used.

Figure 6.3(b) shows a typical family of curves relating collector current I_c, to collector-base voltage, V_{cb}, for various values of emitter current I_e. The curve for $I_e = 0$ is of particular importance. The curve is the reverse characteristic of the base-collector diode. It is in fact the plot of the saturation current I_{co} discussed in the previous section. At room temperature I_{co} has normally a low value of the order of a few microamps. When the temperature rises, I_{co} increases very considerably with the result that the whole family of curves is lifted. It will be noticed that the family of curves is shown in the first quandrant even though V_{cb} is a negative voltage. In order to facilitate calculations and also make for easier comparison with valve characteristics, transistor characteristic curves are usually drawn in the first quadrant regardless

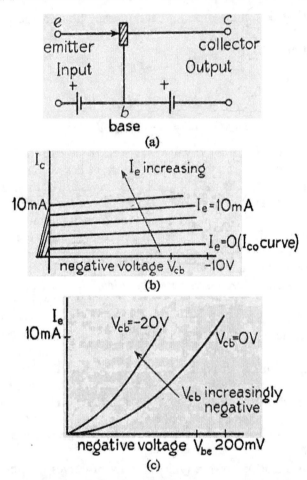

FIG. 6.3. Common base configuration. (a) Basic circuit. (b) Collector current I_c versus collector-base voltage V_{cb} for various values of I_e. (c) Emitter current I_e versus base-emitter voltage V_{be}

of whether the quantities involved are considered as positive or negative. This was not the case with the early works on the subject. In what follows positive current directions are taken as those of the steady d.c. currents which flow under normal operating conditions with suitable bias in the absence of signals.

I_e into the transistor emitter terminal e
I_b out of the transistor base terminal b
I_c out of the transistor collector terminal c.

The above curves do not completely describe transistor behaviour as did the $I_a \sim V_a$ curves for valves. (Although the transfer characteristics of the $I_a \sim V_g$ curves were plotted for valves, their data might have been deduced from the $I_a \sim V_a$ curves.) A second set of curves which shows the non-linear relation between input current and voltage is necessary.

For common base operation the set relating emitter-base voltage to emitter current is used. This is shown at Fig. 6.3(c) for two values of collector-base voltage. It will be seen that the relation is far from linear indicating that the input resistance is non-linear.

Reference to Fig. 6.3(b) indicates that for small signal operation, a current i_e superimposed on the steady current I_e in the emitter circuit which exists by virtue of suitable bias, will produce a small signal i_c superimposed on the steady collector current I_c. Operation will be approximately linear for these signal currents. The current gain will be a little less than unity. However reference to Fig. 6.3(c) in addition to Fig. 6.3(b) shows that one cannot normally expect a linear relation between emitter-base voltage and collector current. This also implies that the relation between emitter-base voltage and an output voltage developed across a load resistor connected in series with the collector is not normally linear. The curves of Fig. 6.3(b) and 6.3(c) serve to emphasize that the transistor is essentially a current device. In order to provide approximately sinusoidal operation for a voltage input signal, for example, it is necessary to arrange that the source resistance is large compared with the transistor input resistance. As a result input current is approximately sinusoidal in spite of the variation of input resistance. Hence the output voltage developed across a load resistor in series with the collector is also approximately sinusoidal.

A wide variety of equivalent circuits are used when considering small signal transistor operation. The voltage form of one such is given in Fig. 6.4. This is the 'equivalent-T' for common-base condition at low frequencies. r_e, r_b, r_c and α are transistor parameters quoted by manufacturers in the same way as valve parameters μ, g_m, and r_a are quoted. r_e, r_b, and r_c are related, but not equal to, the resistances from the appropriate terminals to a point in the base region which is taken to have the potential of point b in Fig. 6.2(b). While there is no standardization as to symbols, those above are widely employed. The derivation of the single voltage generator form of equivalent circuit discussed above from the more precise two-gener-

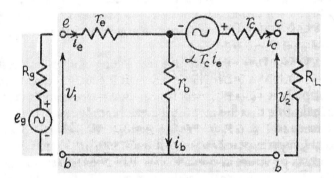

FIG. 6.4. 'Equivalent-T', voltage generator form, for common base operation

ator form is considered in some detail in Ref. 6.2 which also gives the derivation of the other transistor configurations. The single voltage generator in the collector arm which represents transistor action for common base connection has an output proportional to the input current i_e and is of magnitude $\alpha r_c i_e$ volts.

Normally $r_e < r_b < r_c$ and $\alpha \simeq 1$. Typical values might be

$$r_e = 10\Omega$$

$$r_b = 500\Omega$$

$$r_c = 500 \text{ k}\Omega$$

$$\alpha = 0.98$$

The wide variations which occur in the values of the parameters above have a profound effect on transistor circuit performance as will be seen later.

Analysis of the equivalent circuit of Fig. 6.4 yields the following results for low frequencies. The various symbols are indicated on the figure. A complete analysis for each of the three transistor configurations is given in Ref. 6.4.

Input resistance R

$$R_i = r_e + r_b - \frac{r_b(\alpha r_c + r_b)}{R_L + r_b + r_c}$$ 6.3(a)

The input resistance is seen to be a function of the load resistance R_L. This occurs for each of the three transistor configurations. It is not the case with normal valve amplifying stages.

The wide range of values for input resistance is indicated when the extreme cases are considered, and the approximations resulting from the relation $r_e < r_b < r_c$ made.

For $\qquad\qquad R_L = 0, \quad R_i \simeq r_e + (1-\alpha) r_b$ 6.3(b)

For $\qquad\qquad R_L \to \infty, \quad R_i \simeq r_e + r_b$ 6.3(c)

Output resistance R_o

$$R_o = r_c + r_b \left(\frac{r_e + R_g - \alpha r_c}{r_b + r_e + R_g} \right)$$ 6.4(a)

In this case the output resistance R_o is a function of source resistance R_g. Again the dependence occurs for each configuration. Such dependence is not normally the case with valve operation. When

$$R_g = 0, \quad R_o = r_c + r_b \left(\frac{r_e - \alpha r_c}{r_b + r_e} \right)$$ 6.4(b)

$$R_g \to \infty, \quad R_o \simeq r_c + r_b$$ 6.4(c)

Current gain
The current gain is i_c/i_e where

$$\frac{i_c}{i_e} = \frac{\alpha r_c + r_b}{R_L + r_b + r_c}$$ 6.5(a)

Positive directions of currents i_c and i_e are shown in Fig. 6.4. If $R_L \ll r_c$ as is frequently the case,

$$\frac{i_c}{i_e} \simeq \alpha \qquad\qquad 6.5(b)$$

There is no phase reversal between input and output current.

Voltage gain

The voltage gain may be taken as v_2/v_1. Alternatively it may be considered as v_2/e_g, where e_g is the voltage provided by a source of internal resistance R_g. These voltage quantities are shown on the diagram of Fig. 6.4. Analysis of the circuit of Fig. 6.4 yields

$$\frac{v_2}{e_g} = \frac{i_c R_L}{e_g} = \frac{(\alpha r_c + r_b) R_L}{(R_L + r_b + r_c)(r_e + r_b + R_g) - r_b(\alpha r_c + r_b)} \qquad 6.6(a)$$

The expression shows that the voltage gain is related to R_L, R_g, r_e, r_b, r_c, and α. Since r_c is generally much greater than either r_b or r_e, eqn. 6.6(a) may be rewritten,

$$\frac{v_2}{e_g} \simeq \frac{\alpha R_L}{r_e + r_b(1-\alpha) + R_g} \qquad\qquad 6.6(b)$$

Notice that there is no phase reversal between input and output.

At low frequencies negligible phase-shift is introduced with common base operation. A small positive input signal current will result in a small positive output current and vice versa. The configuration has the highest maximum operating frequency of the three possible arrangements. Substitution of values in the above equations shows that common base operation is characterized by low input impedance and high output impedance. Although the current gain is less than unity, a substantial power gain may be possible by virtue of the low input impedance and high output impedance. Voltage gain will be achieved.

(ii) *Common or grounded emitter operation.* Figure 6.5(a) shows the arrangement with the emitter common to both input and output circuits. As before, bias is indicated by batteries. Grounded emitter operation is analogous to grounded cathode valve operation, though as for the grounded base case, there are important differences. Current input signals are applied at the base terminal and outputs taken at the collector terminal. If voltages are considered, then voltage input signals are applied between emitter and base, and output signals are taken across load resistors connected between collector and emitter.

Figure 6.5(b) shows a typical plot of collector current, I_c, as a function of collector-emitter voltage, V_{ce}, for various values of the base current I_b. The $I_b = 0$ curve corresponds to the open-circuit condition for the emitter-base junction. The curve is in fact the plot of the saturation current, I_{co}, for the reverse-bias base-collector junction. Since in this condition no external base current flows, a current of equal magnitude flows to the base from the emitter. As will be seen later in the section a base current I_{co} produces by transistor amplifying action a current in the collector of approximate magnitude,

$$I_{co}\left(\frac{1}{1-\alpha}\right)$$

Hence the total current to the collector will be,

$$I_{co} + \left(\frac{1}{1-\alpha}\right)I_{co} = I_{co}\left(\frac{\alpha}{1-\alpha}\right) = I_{co'}$$

The value of $I_{co'}$ may be as much as a hundred times I_{co}. As for the common-base condition $I_{co'}$ is very sensitive to temperature. As $I_{co'}$ increases the whole family of curves rises as if on a pedestal.

Since the relation between input voltage, V_{be}, and input current, I_b, is non-linear it is necessary to provide the characteristic curves of Fig. 6.5(c) which relate the two quantities for different values of collector-emitter voltage V_{ce}.

Reference to Fig. 6.5(b) shows that for small signal operation, a small positive current i_b superimposed on the steady base current I_b will produce a small positive signal i_c superimposed on the steady collector signal I_c. According to the sign convention adopted for signal currents this implies that a signal which flows in at the base terminal would produce a negative signal at the collector, i.e. sign reversal takes place. The curves of Fig. 6.5(b) indicate that as for the previous case of common base working operation for smal signal currents will be approximately linear. Operation for voltage signals will be approximately linear only if suitable precautions are taken.

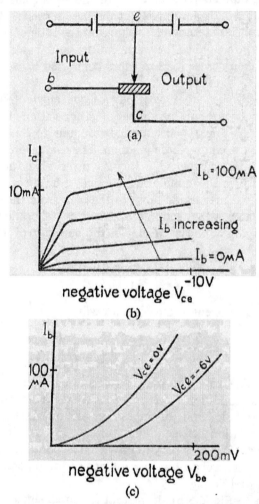

FIG. 6.5. Common emitter configuration. (a) Basic circuit. (b) Collector current I_e versus collector-emitter voltage V_{ee} for various values of I_b. (c) Base current I_b versus base-emitter voltage V_{be}

Analysis of the voltage 'equivalent-T' circuit shown in Fig. 6.6 describes the transistor behaviour at low frequencies. The equivalent voltage generator which appears in the collector arm has an output proportional to the input signal current and equal to $r_c i_b$ volts. The associated resistor in the collector arm is of magnitude r_c/b where

$$b \simeq \frac{1}{1-\alpha}$$

The quantities r_e, r_b, r_c, and α have the same significance and values

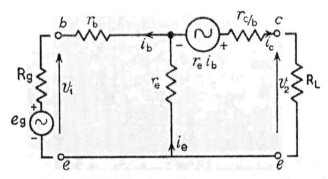

FIG. 6.6. 'Equivalent-T', voltage generator form, for common emitter

as for the previous case. Analysis of the equivalent circuit of Fig. 6.6 gives the following results. The relation $r_e < r_b < r_c$ holds.

Input resistance R_I

$$R_I = r_b + r_e + \frac{r_e b(r_c + r_e)}{r_c + (R_L + r_e)b} \qquad \text{6.7(a)}$$

Two special cases occur,

$$R_L = 0 \quad \text{when} \quad R_I \simeq r_b + br_e \qquad \text{6.7(b)}$$

$$R_L \rightarrow \infty \quad \text{when} \quad R_I \simeq r_b + r_e \qquad \text{6.7(c)}$$

Output resistance R_o

$$R_o = \frac{r_c}{b} + \frac{r_e(r_b + r_c + R_g)}{r_b + r_e + R_g} \qquad \text{6.8(a)}$$

8

When $\qquad R_g = 0, \quad R_o \simeq r_c/b + r_e r_c/r_b \qquad$ 6.8(b)

When $\qquad R_g \to \infty, \quad R_o \simeq r_c/b \qquad$ 6.8(c)

Current gain

The current gain is $\dfrac{\text{signal current out at the collector}}{\text{signal current in at the base}} = \dfrac{i_c}{(-i_b)}$

where the negative sign arises by virtue of the definition of positive current direction. Analysis of the equivalent circuit gives,

$$\frac{i_c}{(-i_b)} = \frac{-b(r_c - r_e)}{r_c + (R_L + r_e)\,b} \qquad \text{6.9(a)}$$

When $\qquad R_L \to 0 \dfrac{i_c}{(-i_b)} \simeq . -b \qquad$ 6.9(b)

but $\qquad b \simeq \dfrac{1}{1 - \alpha}$

hence $\qquad \dfrac{i_c}{(-i_b)} \simeq -\dfrac{1}{1 - \alpha} \qquad$ 6.9(c)

The current gain for common emitter condition is often called β where the strict definition of β is that β is the current gain with collector terminals short circuited. Hence $b = \beta$ for the short circuit condition only.

Voltage gain

$$\frac{v_o}{e_g} = \frac{-b(r_c - r_e)\,R_L}{(r_c + bR_L)(r_b + r_e + R_g) + r_e b(r_b + R_g + r_c)} \qquad \text{6.10}$$

Substitution of typical values in the above equations indicates that common emitter operation is characterized by a moderate to large current gain. This may lie between 10 and 150 for normal transistor types. A useful voltage gain also may be attained. Input and output impedances have moderate values. The maximum operating frequency is considerably less than for common base condition. Phase reversal occurs.

(ii) *Common or grounded collector operation.* Figure 6.7 shows the common collector arrangement with the collector common to input and output circuits. Since operation is analogous to cathode-follower valve operation, the circuit bears the alternative name of emitter follower. Current input signals are applied at the base and output currents are taken at the emitter. Voltage input signals are applied between base and collector, and output signals are taken across load resistors connected between emitter and collector. Performance may

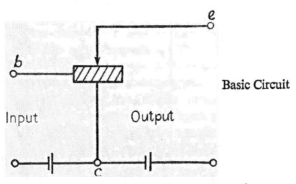

Basic Circuit

FIG. 6.7. Common collector configuration

be estimated by reference to the characteristic curves already considered for grounded base and grounded emitter operation.

Analysis of the voltage 'equivalent-T' circuit of Fig. 6.8 indicates performance at low frequencies. It will be noted that the circuit has certain features in common with common emitter operation. As before

$$b \simeq \frac{1}{1-\alpha} \quad \text{and} \quad r_e < r_b < r_c$$

Input resistance R_i

$$R_i = r_b + r_c \left\{ \frac{(R_L + r_e)(b+1)}{r_c + b(R_L + r_e)} \right\} \qquad 6.11(a)$$

where
$$b \simeq \frac{1}{1-\alpha} \quad \text{and} \quad b+1 \simeq b$$

There are two special cases

$$R_L = 0 \quad \text{when} \quad R_i \simeq r_b + r_e b \qquad \text{6.11(b)}$$

$$R_L \to \infty \quad \text{when} \quad R_i \simeq r_b + r_c \qquad \text{6.11(c)}$$

Output resistance

$$R_o = r_e + \frac{r_c(R_g + R_b)}{r_c(1+b) + b(R_g + r_b)} \quad \text{now normally } b \gg 1$$

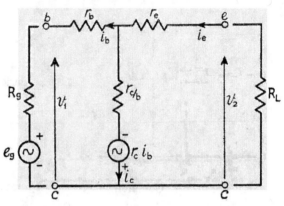

FIG. 6.8. 'Equivalent-T', voltage generator form, for common collector

Hence
$$R_o \simeq r_e + \frac{r_c(R_g + r_b)}{b(r_c + r_b + R_g)} \qquad \text{6.12(a)}$$

When
$$R_g = 0, \quad R_o \simeq r_e + r_b/b \qquad \text{6.12(b)}$$

When
$$R_g \to \infty, \quad R_o \simeq r_e + r_c/b \qquad \text{6.12(c)}$$

Current gain

Reference to Fig. 6.8 shows that current gain is given by

$$\frac{(-i_e)}{(-i_b)} = \frac{i_e}{i_b}$$

where
$$\frac{i_e}{i_b} = \frac{r_c(1+b)}{r_c + b(r_e + R_L)}$$

now $b \gg 1$ and if R_L is of moderate value, as is frequently the case.

$$\frac{i_e}{i_b} \simeq b \qquad\qquad 6.13$$

Voltage gain

Making the usual approximation, $r_e < r_b < r_c$, the voltage gain is given by

$$\frac{v_o}{e_g} \simeq \frac{R_L}{R_L + \dfrac{R_L R_g}{r_c} + \dfrac{R_g}{b}} \qquad\qquad 6.14$$

The common collector circuit is characterized by high input impedance and low output impedance. The current gain is high while the voltage gain, as seen by eqn. 6.14, is less than unity. There is small phase shift between input and output.

The results obtained by the analysis of the transistor equivalent circuits above have been considered in some detail in this section. In the context of a book of this sort, such results are not of the highest importance in themselves. However, in addition to providing some analytical justification for specific transistor properties in the three configurations, they indicate very clearly some of the essential differences between valve and transistor behaviour. As will be seen later they illustrate some of the difficulties associated with the operation of transistor d.c. computing amplifiers.

6.4 Preliminary considerations of transistor computing amplifiers

The use of transistor computing amplifiers rather than valve computing amplifiers for analogue computing purposes offers several substantial advantages providing the performance of the transistor amplifier is adequate. Some of the advantages are summarized below.

(i) *Physical size*. Transistors of the type used for computing purposes occupy a volume very considerably less than valves used for the same purpose. As a result the number of computing units per standard rack may be increased by a factor of several times.

(ii) *Ruggedness*. Transistors are more robust than valves. Current production types tend to be very reliable and have a long life.

(iii) *Power supplies*. Normally transistors work with H.T. voltages of comparatively low value. Heater supplies are no longer required.

Power consumption is much less than with valve operation. A factor of 50:1 might be typical. As a result the working temperature of the machine is little above ambient. Ventilation problems are much

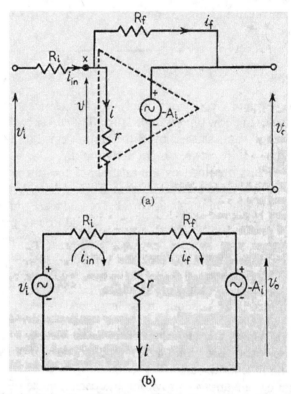

(a)

(b)

FIG. 6.9. Analysis of operational amplifier in terms of transfer impedance. (a) Schematic diagram of gain-change amplifier. (b) Two-mesh equivalent circuit

reduced. The reduction in power requirements brings a large reduction in the overall size of the machine.

The use of transistors, however, provides certain difficulties not encountered with valve operation.

Since the transistor is essentially a current operated device some of the early work describes attempts to employ current rather than voltage as the analogue quantity with transistor computing amplifiers. Hellerman (Ref. 6.5) compares voltage and current computing in a theoretical way. Kerfoot (Ref. 6.6) goes on to consider current computing in greater detail and gives the circuit of a prototype operational amplifier. One major difficulty is the provision of H.T. power supplies for the computing amplifiers which are suitably isolated from ground especially when a capacitor is used as a feedback element. A second difficulty concerns the satisfactory measurement of the signal currents. Other difficulties occur, for example, the calibration of devices intended to fulfil the same function as coefficient potentiometers used in voltage computing would not be easy. For the above and other reasons, voltage has been retained as the analogue quantity with transistor computing amplifiers.

It is convenient to define the gain of a transistor computing amplifier in terms of the voltage output produced by a given input current, i.e. in terms of its transfer impedance (Ref. 6.7). Analysis in terms of transfer impedance for a gain-change amplifier and for an integrator has been considered by Cundall, Saggerson, and Shaw (Ref. 6.8). The case of a gain-change amplifier is discussed below in some detail.

Figure 6.9(a) shows the basic circuit. R_i and R_f are the computing resistors connected in the same manner as those used with valve amplifiers. r is the input resistance of the amplifier in the open-loop condition. If the output impedance is assumed to be small, then the voltage which appears across the output terminals is $(-Ai)$ volts, where $-A$ is the amplifier open-loop transfer impedance, and i is the current which flows in at the first stage of the amplifier. The 180° phase-shift in the amplifier which is implied by the negative sign for the output voltage is necessary to ensure amplifier stability. For the moment drift currents are neglected.

The two-mesh equivalent circuit is shown in Fig. 6.9(b). Consideration of the circulating currents i_{in} and i_f provides the following relations

$$\left. \begin{aligned} v_i &= (R_i+r)\,i_{in} - r i_f \\ Ai &= -v_o = -r i_{in} + (r+R_f)\,i_f \\ i &= i_{in} - i_f \end{aligned} \right\} \qquad 6.15$$

Solution in terms of v_i and v_o yields the result

$$\frac{v_o}{v_i} = -\frac{R_f}{R_i}\left(\frac{1}{1+\dfrac{R_f}{A}\left[1+\left(\dfrac{R_i+R_f}{R_iR_f}\right)r\right]}\right)$$

or

$$\frac{v_o}{v_i} = -\frac{R_f}{R_i}\left(\frac{1}{1+\dfrac{R_f}{A}\left[1+\dfrac{r}{R}\right]}\right) \qquad\qquad 6.16$$

where $R = R_iR_f/(R_i+R_f)$ i.e. R is the parallel combination of R_i and R_f.

In the ideal case

$$\frac{v_o}{v_i} = -\frac{R_f}{R_i} \qquad\qquad 6.17$$

Comparison of eqn. 6.16 and eqn. 6.17 shows that for good approximation to the ideal case, the value of A must be large compared with R_f. In addition it is desirable to have a value of open-loop input resistance r which is small compared sith the parallel combination of R_i and R_f since the transfer impedance is divided by a factor $(1+r/R)$ to yield a modified transfer impedance A'. Provided that $r/R < 1$, $A' \simeq A$. The relation of eqn. 6.16 then becomes,

$$\frac{v_o}{v_i} \simeq -\frac{R_f}{R_i}\left(\frac{1}{1+R_f/A'}\right)$$

Expansion by the binomial theorem gives

$$\frac{v_o}{v_i} \simeq -\frac{R_f}{R_i}\left\{1-\frac{R_f}{A'}+\frac{1}{2}\left(\frac{R_f}{A'}\right)^2+\dots\right\}$$

If $(R_f/A') < 1$ then the percentage error due to the finite value of A' becomes,

$$\frac{R_f}{A}\times 100 \text{ per cent} \qquad\qquad 6.18$$

An integrator is best considered in terms of the general case where computing elements Z_i and Z_f are employed and the analysis is performed using the Laplace transform technique. Relations similar to those of eqn. 6.15, but now in terms of generalized impedances and the transforms of current and voltage quantities, yield the result,

$$\frac{\bar{v}_o}{\bar{v}_i} = \frac{-Z_f(p)}{Z_i(p)} \left\{ \frac{1}{1+\dfrac{Z_f(p)}{A(p)}\left[1+\dfrac{Z_i(p)+Z_f(p)}{Z_i(p)Z_f(p)}.r(p)\right]} \right\}. \qquad 6.19$$

For the case of an integrator,

$$\left. \begin{array}{l} Z_i(p) = R_i \\[2mm] Z_f(p) = \dfrac{1}{pC} \end{array} \right\} \qquad 6.20$$

and

Also $A(p) = A$ and $r(p) = r$ since both are resistive quantities. Hence,

$$\frac{\bar{v}_o}{\bar{v}_i} = \frac{-1}{pCR_i}\left(\frac{1}{1+\dfrac{1}{pCA}\left[1+\dfrac{R_i+1/pC}{R_i/pC}.r\right]}\right)$$

$$= \frac{-1}{pCR_i}\left(\frac{1}{1+\dfrac{1}{pCA}[1+r/R_i+r/A]}\right) \qquad 6.21$$

Now for typical values of r, R_i, and A, $r < R_i$ and $r \ll A$. Hence the term r/A may be neglected and the transfer impedance A considered to be divided by a factor approximately equal to $(1+r/R_i)$ to yield a modified transfer impedance A'. Hence,

$$\frac{\bar{v}_o}{\bar{v}_i} \simeq \frac{-1}{pCR_i}\left[\frac{1}{1+\dfrac{1}{pCA'}}\right]$$

$$= \frac{-1}{pCR_i}\left[\frac{pCA'}{1+pCA'}\right] \qquad 6.22$$

In the ideal case for an integrator

$$\frac{\bar{v}_o}{\bar{v}} = -\frac{1}{pCR_i} \qquad 6.23$$

The term $[pCA'/1+pCA']$ therefore modifies the performance. Consider a step-function input, for example, where the input voltage step is v_i volts. Thus $\bar{v}_i = v_i/p$. Then in eqn. 6.22

$$\bar{v}_o = \frac{v_i}{pCR_i}\left(\frac{CA'}{1+pCA'}\right)$$

Whence

$$v_o = -v_i\frac{t}{CR_i} + v_i\frac{t^2}{2C^2A'R_i} + \dots$$

$$= -v_i\frac{t}{CR_i}\left(1 + \frac{t}{2CA'} + \dots\right) \qquad 6.24$$

Comparison with eqn. 6.23 shows that the percentage error is

$$\frac{t}{2CA'} \times 100 \text{ per cent} \qquad 6.25$$

Equations 6.18 and 6.25 both indicate that for good accuracy a large value of A is necessary. For gain-change a small value of R_i is desirable, while for integration C should have a large value.

Summation has not so far been mentioned. Analysis similar to that used for the gain-change case may be performed to show that summation is possible with transistor amplifiers. It will be seen in the next section that the virtual earth technique is a useful alternative. Equation 6.19 indicates that for more complicated operations the transfer-function approach may be employed.

6.5 The virtual earth principle

The idea of virtual earth operation may be applied to the transistor computing amplifier. Comparison with the valve amplifier is useful at this point. Consider Fig. 6.10(a) which shows a schematic diagram of a valve computing amplifier connected for gain-change. If the input impedance to the amplifier proper is taken as infinite, then the input current i_{in} will flow through the feedback resistor so that

$$i_{in} = i_f = i \qquad 6.26$$

It is instructive to consider the effective closed-loop input impedance R_{eff} at the point A, the virtual earth point. This is given by the relation,

$$R_{\text{eff}} = v_a/i \qquad 6.27$$

where v_a is the potential at the point A, and $i = i_{\text{in}}$. As was seen in Chapter 3,

$$\frac{v_a - v_o}{R} = i \quad \text{and} \quad v_o = -Mv_a$$

Hence

$$R_{\text{eff}} = \frac{v_a}{i} = \frac{R_f}{1+M} \qquad 6.28$$

An equivalent circuit in terms of R_{eff} is shown in Fig. 6.10(b). The departure of the point A from earth potential due to the passage of current i to earth as shown in Fig. 6.10(b) will be very small for practical values of M. As the value of M increases the potential at A more nearly approaches earth potential.

With transistor amplifiers the virtual earth principle again applies. Consider Fig. 6.9(a) once more. v is the potential at the point X at the input to the amplifier. The closed-loop input impedance, R_{eff}, is given by

$$R_{\text{eff}} = v/i_{\text{in}} \qquad 6.29$$

The relations below also apply,

$$\left.\begin{aligned}
v_i - v &= R_i i_{\text{in}} \\
v - v_o &= R_f i_f \\
v_o &= -Ai \\
v &= ir \\
i_{\text{in}} &= i + i_f
\end{aligned}\right\} \qquad 6.30$$

Substitution of the relations of eqn. 6.30 into eqn. 6.29 yields the following result,

$$R_{\text{eff}} = \frac{v}{i_{\text{in}}} = \frac{R_f}{1 + \frac{1}{r}(A + R_f)} \qquad 6.31$$

If $R_f \ll A$ as is usual, then,

$$R_{\text{eff}} \simeq R_f \left(\frac{r}{A}\right) \qquad\qquad 6.32$$

Since $r \ll A$, the potential at point X by virtue of the input current i_{in} will be very small. Point X may be regarded as a virtual earth as

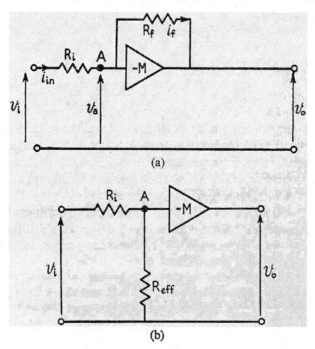

(a)

(b)

Fig. 6.10. Virtual earth approach to valve computing amplifier. (a) Schematic for gain-change configuration. (b) Equivalent circuit

in the valve case. The analysis of a multi-stage amplifier with shunt feedback of the type provided by R_f in the above treatment has been given by Almond and Boothroyd (Ref. 6.9). Their work emphasizes that such feedback results in a very low value for R_{eff}.

When using the virtual earth approach to the valve computing amplifier, the whole of the input current was assumed to flow through the feedback resistor. This led immediately to the result

$$\frac{v_o}{v_i} = -\frac{R_f}{R_i}$$

in the ideal case with an amplifier of infinite voltage gain.

With the transistor amplifier, the relation between the input current i_{in}, the current i into the amplifier proper, and the current i_f through the feedback resistor, is important. Further consideration of the equations of 6.30 gives the result

$$i_f = i_{in}\left(1 - \frac{R_f}{r+A+R_f}\right) \qquad 6.33(a)$$

Since $r < R_f \ll A$

$$i_f \simeq i_{in}\left(1 - \frac{R_f}{A}\right) \qquad 6.33(b)$$

In the ideal case when $A \to \infty$

$$i_f = i_{in} \qquad 6.34$$

It must be emphasized that this rather surprising result is a consequence of the feedback which has been applied. The result is the same as the ideal condition for valve operation. Coupled with the idea of the virtual earth principle, eqn. 6.34 leads, as in the valve case, to the immediate result,

$$\frac{v_o}{v_i} = -\frac{R_f}{R_i}$$

This is the same as that given in eqn. 6.17.

Finally consider the current i. This is given by the relation,

$$i = i_{in} - i_f = \frac{R_f i_{in}}{r+A+R_f} \qquad 6.35(a)$$

Again $r < R_f \ll A$ in practice, hence

$$i \simeq \frac{R_f}{A} i_{in} \qquad 6.35(b)$$

The analysis above affords a most interesting comparison between valve and transistor computing amplifiers. Consideration of the amplifiers in terms of voltage gain and transfer impedance respectively shows that the virtual earth principle, with associated low input impedance at the virtual earth point, is applicable in each case. The notion that in the ideal case because the current flowing through the feedback computing resistance is equal to the current through the input computing resistance the ratio v_o/v_i is determined solely by the ratio R_f/R_i, is common to both.

The analysis can be extended to the general case for input computing element Z_i and feedback element Z_f by the use of the Laplace transform technique.

6.6 Drift in transistor computing amplifiers

In Section 6.3, it was shown that drift currents rather than drift voltages are important when considering the behaviour of transistor stages. Drift currents were seen to be functions of temperature and to have a constant value for any particular temperature. Changes in the value of V_{be} also result in drift currents.

When using transistor computing amplifiers, a current is injected at the input to the amplifier proper in the zero set condition to provide zero output voltage when the input resistor R_i is earthed. The value of this current is equal in magnitude and opposite in sign to the 'drift current referred to input'. In the ideal case where the ambient temperature is fixed, the adjustment should prove sufficient providing the power supplies and component values are stable. In practice the value of ambient temperature will vary. As a result the drift current will change and an output drift voltage occur. As with valve amplifiers drift at the first stage is all important. Figure 6.11 shows how I_{co} and $I_{co'}$ vary with temperature for a typical low power transistor. It will be noticed that I_{co} and $I_{co'}$ both double in value for an increase in temperature of rather less than 10°C. Typical values of $I_{co'}$ for common transistors of the type employed for computing amplifiers might be between 10 μA and 100μA at 25°C. It is instructive to determine the relation betweeen a drift current i_d and the corresponding drift voltage at the output of a computing amplifier.

Consider first a computing amplifier arranged for gain-change. The equivalent circuit is shown in Fig. 6.12. Resistor R_l is earthed at the

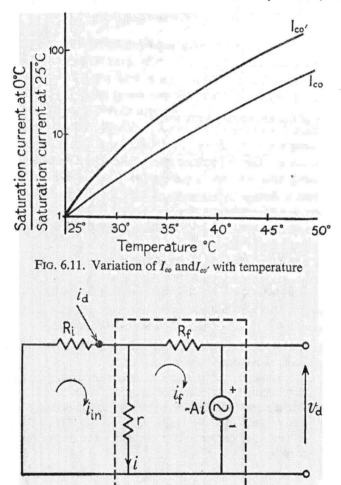

FIG. 6.11. Variation of I_{co} and $I_{co'}$ with temperature

FIG. 6.12. Drift current in transistor amplifier

end remote from the amplifier. This implies zero input voltage v_l. The currents i_{in}, i_f, and i which flow in the circuit do so by virtue of the drift current alone. This is represented by a current source i_d at the input to the amplifier proper. The following relations hold for the equivalent circuit of Fig. 6.12.

$$
\left.\begin{aligned}
0 &= i_{\text{in}}(R_l+r)-i_dR_l-ri_f \\
Ai &= -i_{\text{in}}r+i_f(R_f+r) \\
Ai &= -v_d \\
i &= i_{\text{in}}-i_f
\end{aligned}\right\}
\qquad 6.36
$$

Solution of the above yields the result,

$$
\begin{aligned}
v_d &= -\left\{\frac{AR_fR_i}{R_lR_f+R_lr+R_fr+R_lA}\right\}i_d \\
&= -\left\{\frac{R_f}{1+R_f/A\left[1+\left(\dfrac{R_f+R_l}{R_fR_i}\right)r\right]}\right\}i_d \\
&= -\left\{\frac{R_f}{1+R_f/A[1+r/R]}\right\}i_d \qquad 6.37
\end{aligned}
$$

where
$$
R = \frac{R_fR_l}{R_f+R_l}
$$

Provided $r/A < 1$ and $R_f < A$, the output drift voltage is given by the approximate relation

$$
v_d \simeq -R_f i_d \qquad 6.38
$$

This implies that the drift voltage, v_d, is minimized by the use of a feedback resistor of low value.

The analysis can be extended to the general case for input computing element Z_i and feedback element Z_f. The case of an integrator, for example, has been considered by the authors of Ref. 6.8. For a drift current i_d, the equivalent input voltage is i_dR_l. Hence the output drift voltage, v_d, after t seconds, produced by a constant drift current i_d, is given by

$$
v_d \simeq -\frac{(i_dR_l)}{R_lC}\int_0^t dt = i_dR_l\frac{t}{T} \qquad 6.39
$$

where T is the time constant $R_i C$. Equation 6.39 implies that best drift performance for a particular value of T occurs when R_i is as small as possible, and C is as large as possible.

6.7 Transistor computing amplifiers in practice

Since transistors have been applied to computing techniques only recently, circuit designs have not yet settled into a definite pattern, as is the case with valve operation. Therefore a detailed treatment of transistor circuits cannot be attempted.

As was mentioned in Section 6.4 some of the early work on transistor computing amplifiers concerned the development of current-operated amplifiers (Ref. 6.5 and 6.6). However, for the reasons mentioned in that section, voltage has been retained as the analogue quantity.

One possible technique for the design of a transistor operational amplifier is to endeavour to produce a transistor circuit which has an open-loop performance as similar as possible to the corresponding valve circuit. To achieve this end a transistor amplifier which has properties similar to those discussed at the beginning of Chapter 3 is required. High input impedance, large voltage gain, and overall phase reversal are especially important.

As was shown in Section 6.3(iii) and eqn. 6.11 a common collector (emitter follower) circuit has the property of high input impedance if the load resistance has a large value. No phase reversal occurs. If two or more emitter follower circuits are arranged in cascade, the input impedance rises further. Equation 6.14 indicates that the voltage gain of such stages is less than unity. A high voltage gain for the whole amplifier may be achieved by the use of a sufficient number of suitable transistor stages. While eqn. 6.6 of Section 6.3 shows that operation in the common base configuration provides a useful voltage gain, no phase reversal occurs. An amplifier consisting of an initial common collector stage followed by common base stages would not exhibit therefore the overall phase reversal necessary for amplifier operation. Interstage matching for a series of common base stages with their low input and high output impedances (eqn. 6.3 and eqn. 6.4) is unsatisfactory in that it results in a loss of voltage gain.

However, common emitter stages provide both current and voltage gain (eqn. 6.9 and eqn. 6.10), a phase reversal, and have input and

9

output impedances of moderate value (eqn. 6.7 and eqn. 6.8). As a result such stages have been preferred to common base stages.

In practice considerations of the stability of the overall amplifier restricted the number of stages which could be used especially in view of the limited frequency response of the transistors used in the early work. Drift problems also restricted the overall gain.

Ettinger (Ref. 6.10) in July 1955 described two computing amplifiers built with the above criteria in mind. The need for as high an input impedance as possible was specifically mentioned. The use of computing resistances of lower value than was normal with valve amplifiers was suggested as a possible method of minimizing the limitations of finite amplifier input impedance. One amplifier had an open-loop voltage gain of 500 and consisted of an input grounded collector stage followed by a grounded base stage and a final grounded emitter stage. Phase reversal considerations dictated the use of a common base rather than common emitter configuration as a second stage. A second amplifier had a gain of 2500 and consisted of a grounded collector stage followed by three grounded emitter stages. Moderate drift performance was attained with each amplifier.

In March 1956 Blecher (Ref. 6.11) discussed the performance of a transistor summing amplifier employed three common emitter stages. Local feedback was applied to the second stage to provide a measure of control over the open-loop gain. Selected transistors were used.

In November 1956 W. A. Curtin (Ref. 6.12) described a simple experimental 5-stage a.c. transistor computing amplifier designed for carrier frequency applications. In order to provide a measure of control over the variation of open-loop gain due to differences between individual transistors, component tolerances, temperature variations and the like, local feedback was applied to each stage. Common emitter stages were used throughout the amplifier. A voltage open-loop gain of 1000 was attained. The amplifier was used to sum two 400 c/s input signals with unity closed-loop gain. The maximum error was ± 0.1 per cent when the loop gain was subject to 50 per cent variation.

A very much more elaborate computing amplifier was described by W. Hochwald and F. H. Gerhard in 1958 (Ref. 6.13). This amplifier used a total of 18 transistors and achieved drift correction with a transistor chopper circuit and associated auxiliary amplifiers. Voltage gain was once more emphasized. An open-loop voltage gain at d.c. of 18×10^6 was quoted for the amplifier. It was pointed out however that for 'high accuracy applications, d.c. input current sensitivities in the region of 100 μμA are required with a dynamic output range of the order of ± 50 volts'. Such values imply a transfer impedance of the order of 5×10^5 MΩ.

The circuits considered above were based, for the most part, on attempts to use techniques resulting from criteria which had proved appropriate to valve operational amplifiers. Section 6.4 however shows that when transistor computing amplifiers are used an analysis in terms of transfer impedance is convenient. Equation 6.16 indicates that this leads to the unexpected result that for transistor amplifiers a low open-loop input resistance is desirable. Under such circumstances the percentage error is given by the relation of eqn. 6.18,

$$\text{percentage error} = \frac{R_f}{A} \times 100 \text{ per cent}$$

where A is the transfer impedance. This relation indicates the need for a large value of transfer impedance.

The papers of Chaplin and Owens published in 1958 are of interest in that they indicate a considerable development in transistor computing amplifiers.

Their first paper (Ref. 6.14) discussed input stages for high-gain d.c. amplifiers. After consideration of the causes of drift in a common emitter stage, drift compensation by the use of a balanced circuit of the long-tail pair type was discussed. This involved the use of matched transistors and considerable care in balancing the amplifier if good results were to be attained. An amplifier in which low-level d.c. signals were converted first into a.c. signals using a modulator, then amplified, and finally rectified to provide an amplified d.c. output was discussed in detail. The process was similar to that employed with the auxiliary amplifiers considered in Chapter 5.6 though transistors rather than relays were used as switches. The drift performance of such modulated amplifiers used as input stages was shown to be substantially better than that of the same transistors used in balanced circuits of conventional type.

The second paper of Chaplin and Owens (Ref. 6.7) considered a complete transistor high-gain chopper-type d.c. amplifier using the circuits discussed in the first paper. A chopping frequency of 1600 c/s was used. The concept of gain expressed in terms of transfer impedance was introduced. The a.c. amplifier used four transistors and had a gain of 20 V/μA over a frequency range 60 c/s–20 kc/s. Considerable care was taken to ensure that the open-loop gain was substantially constant by the provision of local feedback over pairs of transistor stages. D.c. feedback applied to the whole a.c. amplifier was used to stabilize the operating point of the first stage. D.c. feedback was also provided over the complete amplifier. The open-loop gain of the whole system, including the gain achieved at the input chopper was 50 V/μA, or 50 MΩ, over the range from d.c. to 25c/s. The transistors used were chosen at random. Wide tolerance components were employed. The voltage drift referred to the input was less than 100 μV over the range 20°C–50°C. This drift performance compares favourably with the best performance of valve amplifiers.

Further progress was achieved by Cundall, Saggerson, and Shaw (Ref. 6.8). In a paper presented at the International Convention on Transistors and Associated Semiconductor Devices in 1959 a transistor d.c. amplifier designed specifically for use in analogue computers was considered. This paper is of considerable interest in that a complete analysis of the application of transistors to analogue computing amplifiers was given. It began with a detailed analysis of the transistor operational amplifier when used for summation and for integration. The results of this analysis are given in Section 6.4. The characteristics required for a computing accuracy of better than 0.1 per cent per stage were specified. To meet these requirements a complete amplifier incorporating drift correction was described. The d.c. amplifier had a transfer impedance of 1000 V/μA (1000 MΩ) and gave an output swing of $\pm$30 V into a 10 kΩ load. It comprised five d.c. stages with local feedback to minimize the effect of transistor parameter changes. After discussion of various methods of drift correction, that considered in Chapter 5.6 was chosen. The amplifier used for this purpose was based on the design of Chaplin and Owens given above.

A table at the end of the paper summarized the performance of the amplifier and compared it with the performance of a typical valve amplifier. This comparison indicates that a transistor amplifier can attain a performance comparable with that of a valve amplifier provided lower ohmic values of computing resistors, and smaller computing voltages than for valve operation, are acceptable. Drift performance is seen to be comparable with that of a valve amplifier. The transistor amplifier offers substantial advantages as to low volume, low power consumption and negligible heat dissipation.

Amplifiers of the above type have been used by the authors in an analogue computer with complete success. Analogue computers using transistor operational amplifiers are now available commercially.

REFERENCES

6.1. SHOCKLEY, W. 'Transistor physics (forty-sixth Kelvin lecture)', *Proc. I.E.E.*, **103B**, 23, 1956.

6.2. DEWITT, D., and ROSSOFF, A. L. *Transistor Electronics*, McGraw-Hill, New York, 1957.

6.3. HURLEY, R. B. *Junction Transistor Electronics*, John Wiley, New York, 1960.

6.4. AMOS, S. W. *Principles of Transistor Circuits*, Iliffe, London, 1959.

6.5. HELLERMAN, H. 'Some transistor building blocks for analogue computers', *A.I.E.E. Trans.*, **73**, Part 1, 410, 1954.

6.6. KERFOOT, B. P. 'Transistors in current-analog computing', *I.R.E. Transactions on Electronic Computers*, **86**, 1956.

6.7. CHAPLIN, G. B. B., and OWENS, A. R. 'A transistor high-gain chopper-type d.c. amplifier', *Proc. I.E.E.*, **105B**, 258, 1958.

6.8. CUNDALL, C. M., SAGGERSON, J. K., and SHAW, G. 'A transistor d.c. amplifier for use in analogue computers', *Proc. I.E.E.*, **106B**, Suppl. No. 18, 1354, 1959.

6.9. ALMOND, J., and BOOTHROYD, A. R. 'Broadband transistor feedback amplifiers', *Proc. I.E.E.*, **103B**, 93, 1956.

6.10. ETTINGER, G. M. 'Transistor amplifiers for analogue computers', *Electronics*, **28**, 119, July 1955.

6.11. BLECHER, F. H. 'Transistor circuits for Analog and digital systems', *Bell Syst. tech. J.*, **35**, 295, 1956.

6.12. CURTIN, W. A. 'Use of junction transistors in computer amplifiers', *Electrical Engineering (A.I.E.E.)*, **75**, 1011, 1956.

6.13. HOCHWALD, W., and GERHARD, F. W. 'A drift compensated operational amplifier employing a low level silicon transistor chopper', *Proc. Nat. Electronics Conf.*, **14**, 798, 1958.

6.14. CHAPLIN, G. B. B., and OWENS, A. R. 'Some transistor input stages for high-gain d.c. amplifiers', *Proc. I.E.E.*, **105B**, 249, 1958.

CHAPTER 7

Computer Auxiliary Equipment

7.1 Introduction

The analogue computing equipment described in the chapters above suffices for the solution of a wide variety of problems. Additional items of equipment however are frequently required to permit the solution of further classes of problems or provide input and output facilities for analogue computers. This chapter is devoted to a survey of some of these items with brief explanations as to their applications. This survey does not set out to be exhaustive since references to the sources of further information are given.

7.2 Multipliers

The approach to the solution of problems via the use of operational amplifiers made no provision for the multiplication of two independent variables. Sometimes it is necessary to perform such multiplication. This might occur, for example, in the solution of problems in aerodynamics (Ref. 7.1).

In such problems the magnitudes of the aerodynamic derivatives, yaw moment per unit rudder angle for example, determine the forces and moments acting on an aircraft. For a simple representation of the problem such derivatives may be considered as constants, and may be set into the problem as coefficient potentiometer settings. In fact however, the derivatives vary with altitude, temperature, and the like, and thus, in a more sophisticated solution, should change continuously. Such variation normally involves the multiplication of two independent variables.

Various types of multipliers are discussed below.

7.2.1 *Electromechanical multipliers*

Electromechanical multipliers give satisfactory performance providing they are not required to operate at frequencies greater than a few cycles per second.

127

A block diagram of such a multiplier is shown in Fig. 7.1. The multiplier is essentially a high-performance position servomechanism. The servo motor turns the output shaft through an angle θ which is proportional to one of the input quantities v_1. The servomechanism is designed in such a manner that the correct output shaft angle is taken up precisely and with rapid response.

To this end a precision potentiometer is mounted on the output

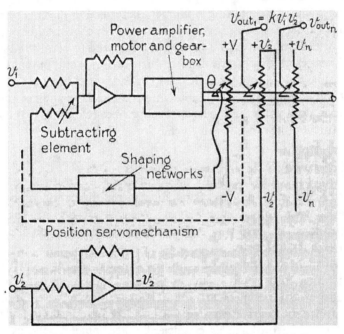

FIG. 7.1. Block diagram of electromechanical multiplier

shaft. This potentiometer is such that the resistance/unit angle of track is a constant. Voltages $+V$ volts and $-V$ volts are applied to the ends of the potentiometer. A negative feedback signal is taken from the slider of the potentiometer to a summing amplifier which provides an error signal to drive the servo motor via the power amplifier. When the voltage at the slider equals v_1 volts, the error signal is zero, and the correct position has been attained. The performance of the position servomechanism is frequently improved by the insertion of shaping networks in the feedback path to ensure rapid response and minimum positional error. Such techniques are discussed at length in Ref. 7.2.

The slider of a second precision potentiometer is mounted on the output shaft. An input voltage v_2, proportional to the other independent variable, is applied to one end of the potentiometer. The same voltage v_2 is also applied to a sign reversing amplifier, and thence, as $-v_2$, to the other end of the potentiometer. The output of the multiplier, v_{out}, is taken from the slider of this potentiometer.

Consideration of Fig. 7.1 shows that the output voltage v_{out} is proportional to θ and also to the voltage v_2. In fact,

$$v_{out} \propto \theta v_2$$

or
$$v_{out} = k v_1 v_2 \qquad 7.1$$

This relation is valid for both positive and negative values of v_1 and v_2. Several precision potentiometers may be ganged together on the output shaft. If voltages $\pm v_3, \pm v_4, \ldots, \pm v_n$ are applied to the ends of such potentiometers, then the output of the nth potentiometer will be

$$v_{n\,out} = k v_1 v_n \qquad 7.2$$

The performance of such electromechanical multipliers depends on the quality of the precision potentiometers and upon the frequency response of the position servomechanisms. Typical specifications for modern equipment quote accuracies of the order of 0·5 per cent and satisfactory operation up to 10 c/s. It will be noticed that the frequency response is limited to a comparatively low value. In the two methods of multiplication to be described below considerably higher frequency responses may be attained.

7.2.2 Quarter square multiplier

The technique appears to have been first mentioned by Chance in 1951 (Ref. 7.3). The principle of operation of the quarter square multiplier is based on the relation

$$\tfrac{1}{4}\{(v_1+v_2)^2-(v_1-v_2)^2\} = v_1 v_2 \qquad 7.3\text{(a)}$$

Figure 7.2 shows how the relation of eqn. 7.3 is achieved. The voltages $+v_1$ and $+v_2$ are applied to a summing amplifier to yield v_1+v_2, and then to a squaring circuit to provide $(v_1+v_2)^2$. Voltages

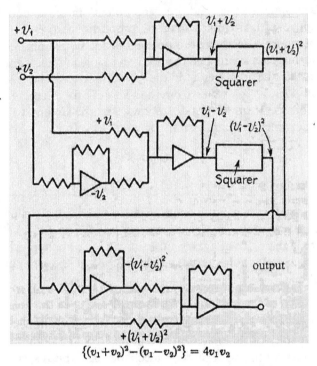

$$\{(v_1+v_2)^2-(v_1-v_2)^2\} = 4v_1v_2$$

FIG. 7.2. Block diagram of quarter-square multiplier

$+v_1$ and $-v_2$ are summed and squared to give $(v_1-v_2)^2$. After sign reversal $(v_1-v_2)^2$ is added to $(v_1+v_2)^2$ to give

$$(v_1+v_2)^2-(v_1-v_2)^2 = 4v_1v_2 \qquad 7.3(b)$$

The scaling of the system is adjusted to provide any convenient overall gain and thus the factor 4 in eqn. 7.3(b) is unimportant.

Squaring is achieved using a series of diodes each biased so that

conduction is initiated for a different level of input voltage in each case. The principle of operation of the squarer is discussed below.

Consider for example the characteristic curve for a typical thermionic diode shown in Fig. 7.3(a). An idealized curve is shown in

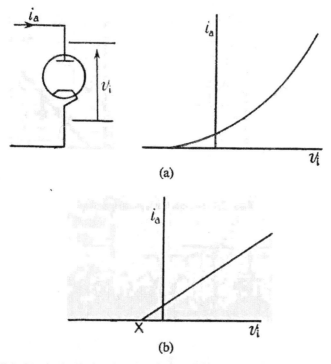

(a)

(b)

FIG. 7.3. Typical diode characteristics. (a) Typical $i_a \sim v_i$ curve. (b) Idealized $i_a \sim v_i$ curve

Fig. 7.3(b). It is seen that conduction does not take place when the anode voltage is substantially below that of the cathode, but that for a value of anode voltage a little less than that of the cathode (about 1 volt) conduction commences. Thereafter there is an approximately straight line relationship between anode current i_a and the applied voltage v_i. The point at which conduction is initiated is the breakpoint, shown at X on the diagram. The forward resistance of the thermionic diode is of the order of 100 Ω while the resistance in the reverse direction may be considered as infinite.

If a bias voltage is applied to the anode of the diode, then the posi-

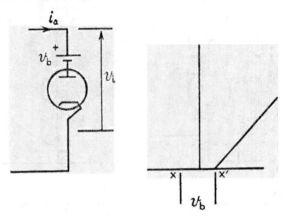

FIG. 7.4 Diode with positive bias

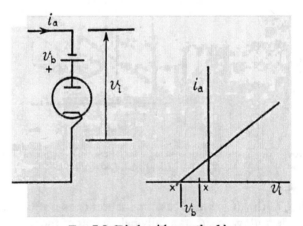

FIG. 7.5. Diode with negative bias

tion of the break-point may be varied at will. Consider for example Fig. 7.4. Here the break-point has been moved to the right through a distance v_b to the point X' by the application of a battery bias voltage

v_b volts. Similarly the break-point may be moved through a distance v_b to the left to point X'' by the application of a bias voltage v_b of opposite polarity as shown in Fig. 7.5. Figure 7.6(a) shows two diodes, biased by different voltages, v_{b_1} and v_{b_2}. In Fig. 7.6(b) the currents i_{a_1}, and i_{a_2} and the total current $i = i_{a_1} + i_{a_2}$ each plotted against applied voltage v_i are shown.

A series of diodes, half biased in the positive direction and half in the negative direction, yields a plot such as that shown in Fig. 7.7.

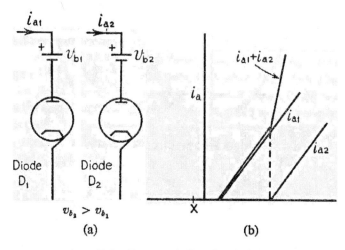

FIG. 7.6. Characteristics of two diodes

It will be seen that providing a reasonable number of diodes are used, the straight line segments approximate to a parabola. The approximation becomes more close as the number of segments is increased.

Figure 7.7 indicates that to perform the operation of squaring, a set of biased diodes may be used. The input voltage v_i is applied to all the diodes simultaneously. The sum of the currents from the diodes obeys the relation

$$\sum i_{an} \simeq k_1 v_i^2 \qquad\qquad 7.4$$

where k_1 is a constant. The currents may be summed conveniently by connecting the cathodes of the diodes via resistors to the virtual earth point of an operational amplifier arranged for summing as shown in Fig. 7.8 whence

$$i = -\frac{v_o}{R} = \sum i_{an} \qquad\qquad 7.5$$

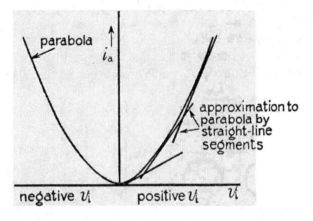

biased-diode circuits

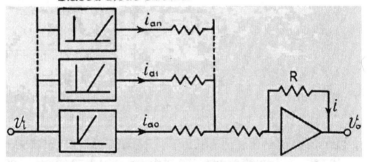

FIG. 7.7. Characteristics for a set of diodes used for squaring

where i is the current flowing through the amplifier feedback resistor R, and v_o is the output voltage. Hence

$$v_o \simeq -k_2 v_i^2 \qquad\qquad 7.6$$

where k_2 is a second constant.

Typical accuracies claimed by manufacturers are of the order of 0·5 per cent of full scale with a useful operating frequency extending to 100 c/s. Batteries are not employed to provide bias voltages in practice. Resistor networks are frequently used however. Crystal diodes too are also often used in place of thermionic diodes in order to utilize their obvious advantages of small size, robust construction, and low power consumption.

7.2.3. Hall-effect multiplier

Consider the diagram of Fig. 7.8. This shows a block of semiconductor material, typically indium arsenide. If a current flows between one pair of faces, and a magnetic field exists across a second pair of faces, then an e.m.f. appears across the faces mutually perpendicular to the first two sets. This phenomenon is the Hall effect (Ref. 7.4). The Hall effect has been known for some considerable time (1879) but was utilized for multiplication in analogue computing only comparatively recently (Ref. 7.5).

The relation between Hall voltage, plate current and magnetic flux density is given by

$$V_H = \frac{R}{t} BI \times 10^{-4} \, \text{mV} \qquad\qquad 7.7$$

where

V_H = Hall voltage in mV

R = Hall coefficient in cm³/coulomb

I = plate current in mA

B = magnetic flux density in weber/metre²

t = plate thickness in cm

If the magnetic flux is derived from a coil carrying a current, the Hall voltage will be proportional to the product of the plate current and the coil current. Thus when input signal currents x and y are applied to the plate and coil respectively, the output Hall voltage is proportional to the product xy. Since in practice signal quantities in analogue computers are voltages, Hall effect multipliers usually incorporate suitable preamplifiers having a high input impedance, and capable of delivering currents to the plate and coil from high impedance, non-reactive, sources. The high input impedance of such amplifiers ensures that the multiplier does not load appreciably the preceding equipment. The high output impedance ensures that the

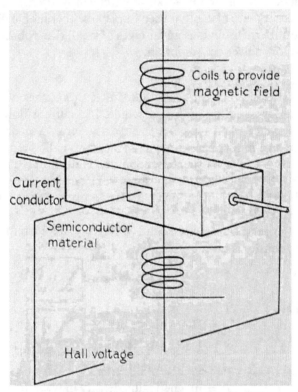

FIG. 7.8. Block diagram to illustrate Hall effect

input currents are proportional to the voltages to be multiplied even though the input impedances presented by the Hall plate, and in particular the coil, may vary.

The frequency response of the Hall effect itself is very high. The frequency response of the multiplier is limited by the response of the associated circuits.

As seen from eqn. 7.7, the Hall voltage is proportional to magnetic flux density and plate current. Any non-linearity in the relation between coil current and magnetic flux density therefore results in a departure from linearity in the multiplier itself. This non-linearity may be considered in terms of the hysteresis loop of the magnetic circuit. The narrower the loop, the better the linearity. Experiments by Chasmar show that the greater the gap in the magnetic circuit in which the Hall plate is situated, the more near linear is the relation between coil current and flux density.

In practice, the above and other practical problems have been overcome to the extent that for a typical multiplier available commercially the frequency response extends from d.c. to 100 c/s with an overall accuracy and linearity of better than ± 0.5 per cent of full scale. Either transistor or valve circuits are used for the input amplifiers. An output amplifier may also be used to obtain a voltage output of convenient amplitude.

7.2.4 *Other multipliers*
The multipliers described in the above sections do not constitute the whole range of available types. While they represent popular techniques others have been, and are, used with success. Two of these are briefly discussed below.

(i) *The crossed-fields multiplier* (Ref. 7.6). This utilizes a special cathode-ray tube fitted with electrostatic deflection plates and an axial coil. Photocells are mounted in front of the screen of the cathode-ray tube on either side of a blank portion of the screen. Signals from the photocells are taken to a difference amplifier the output voltage of which is applied to one pair of deflector plates. The feedback signal is in such a sense that the horizontal deflection of the electron beam is small and confined to the area behind the mask. Under these circumstances it may be shown that the voltage applied to these plates is proportional to the product of the voltage applied to the other pair and the currents through the axial coil. A frequency response extending well beyond 1 kc/s is claimed for the device.

(ii) *Variable mark/space multiplier*. With this technique a rectangular wave is modulated such that the mark/space ratio is proportional to one input voltage, and the amplitude of the wave is proportional to the

10

other input voltage. It may be shown that the mean value of the resulting waveform is proportional to the product of the two input voltages. Details of the development of this technique with diagrams of the appropriate circuits may be found in Ref. 7.10.

7.3 Function generators

In many applications of analogue computers it is necessary to generate a voltage which varies with respect to an input voltage in such a manner that the normal operational amplifier techniques cannot be employed to provide the function. Such functions include sines and cosines, parabolas, and others which may conveniently be expressed as

$$v_o = f(v_i) \qquad\qquad 7.8$$

where f is some function of v_i.

Often such a relation may have been determined from some experiment. For example the results of wind-tunnel tests on an aircraft model might require incorporation in an analogue computer study. Alternatively it might be necessary to provide a function which represents non-linear behaviour of some mechanical device. The generation of such functions, other than sines and cosines which will be considered separately, is discussed below.

Biased diodes were used in the quarter square multiplier discussed in Section 7.2.2 to provide the squaring action necessary for the operation of the multiplier. The use of diodes in this manner is not restricted to the generation of a parabolic characteristic. Provided a reasonable number of diodes are employed, a wide variety of single-valued functions may be produced by this technique. Commercial function generators using this principle are widely used. A typical equipment incorporates twenty diodes, and makes provision for manual adjustment of the resistors used to provide the appropriate bias arrangements. In most cases both positive and negative input voltages are acceptable. Such a function generator will have a frequency response similar to that of a quarter square multiplier. The accuracy with which the function is generated depends on the function itself, and on the number of diodes available. Figure 7.9 illustrates a single-valued function represented by twenty straight-line segments provided by a diode function generator.

While biased diode function generators are used very widely, there are other types. Some are of historical interest only, others are still used.

A potentiometer with a number of tapping points may form a function generator. A schematic diagram of a section of such a device is shown in Fig. 7.10. The voltage between any pair of tapping points has a linear relation, the slope of which is determined by adjustment of the potential between the points. The output voltage is taken at a slider which is made to rotate at a steady rate. A rate servo-

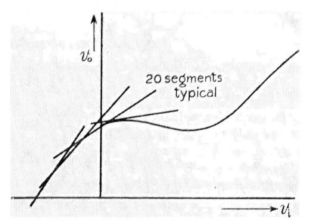

FIG. 7.9. Use of biased diodes to generate $v_o = f(v_i)$

mechanism may be used to ensure that the performance is adequate. Such a function generator may give good results, but it suffers from the limitation of electromechanical devices. The subject is discussed further in Ref. 7.8.

The cathode-ray tube function generator is now of historical interest only. It does not appear to have been used in Britain for several years. The technique was invented independently by Mynall (Ref. 7.9) and McKay (Ref. 7.10) in 1946. An opaque mask was cut to the shape of the function required and attached to the front of the cathode-ray tube. A photocell was mounted in front of the mask. X deflection was provided by a conventional linear timebase. Signals from the photocell, after suitable amplification, were applied to the

10*

Y plates of the tube. These feedback signals were applied in such a way that the fluorescent spot on the screen was constrained to ride the

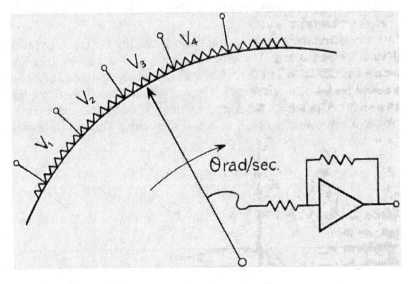

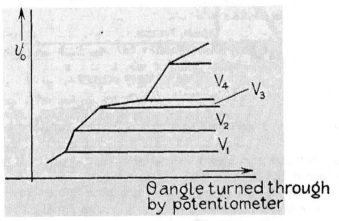

FIG. 7.10. Tapped potentiometer used as function generator

edge of the mask as it moved in the horizontal direction at a steady rate. The voltage at the Y plates was thus proportional to the shape of the function and was taken as the output. Although the frequency response was adequate for many purposes, difficulty was experienced in generating functions with steep slopes and sudden changes of direction.

In various other function generators the function is first drawn out on a cylinder or flat sheet, often in conducting ink. When it is necessary to generate the function, the graph is traced out by some form of sensing device. The output at every instant is taken as a voltage proportional to the displacement of the sensing head from some datum. A wide variety of function generators of this and other types is described in Ref. 7.11.

7.4 Generation of sines and cosines

Sines and cosines may be generated comparatively readily through the use of special potentiometers. These are of two main types.

In one, fine resistance wire is wound on a flat card in a uniform manner. Equal positive and negative voltages are applied to the ends of the wire. The output is taken at a slider which may be rotated about point O at the centre of the card as shown in Fig. 7.11. The voltage at points along the axis Ox varies in a linear fashion. The potential at the slider when it is arranged at an angle θ to the reference axis is given by the approximate relation,

$$v_o \simeq krV\cos\theta \qquad\qquad 7.9$$

where k is a constant and r is the length of the slider arm. The departure from the precise relation is due to the volt drop in the length of wire between the slider and the axis Ox. With fine wire such a volt drop is small.

The addition of a second slider having an arm equal in length to the first permits the generation of the function,

$$v_o' \simeq krV\sin\theta \qquad\qquad 7.10$$

Inspection of Fig. 7.11 indicates that the sine/cosine potentiometer gives an output of the appropriate sign in each of the four quadrants.

In the other principal type of sine/cosine generator, the potentiometer is wound on a card shaped as shown in Fig. 7.12. The lower edge takes the form of a sinewave. Voltages proportional to sines and cosines may then be picked off at the two sliders arranged at right

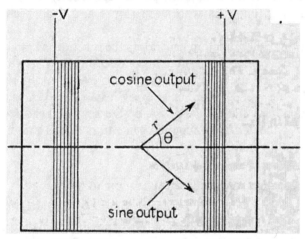

FIG. 7.11. Flat card sine/cosine potentiometer

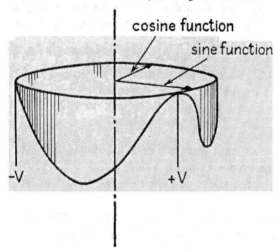

FIG. 7.12. Shaped card sine/cosine potentiometer

angles which make contact with the upper edge of the potentiometer winding.

In each case continuous rotation is possible. However, both suffer from the limitations of electromechanical devices. For example when it is necessary to use a sine/cosine potentiometer in conjunction with a position servomechanism, the frequency response is severely limited.

7.5 Converter devices

With the rapid growth in the application of digital computing techniques it has become increasingly important to be able to convert analogue information to the corresponding digital form and vice versa.

For example one of the more recent applications where this is necessary is in the combined analogue-digital simulator (Ref. 7.12). Here the analogue section of the equipment acts as a model of some physical system, a chemical plant perhaps. Appropriate analogue-to-digital converters provide the digital equivalent of the various voltages in the analogue machine which are proportional to the parameters indicating the performance of the plant. These would include the analogue representations of flow quantities, pressures and temperatures at various points in the system.

This digital information is supplied to a digital computer sufficiently fast in operation to provide a very rapid assessment of performance. Such a machine may well be the prototype of the digital computer which will be used later to control the real plant. The digital machine has as its output control signals which modify the performance of the model of the plant in the light of this assessment to permit optimum operation. These control signals require conversion to the corresponding analogue quantities in the analogue computer. For this purpose digital-to-analogue converters are required.

Most digital computers work in the binary rather than the decimal system. Systems of numbers can be expressed in the form of a series thus,

$$a_n b^n + a_{n-1} b^{n-1} + a_{n-2} b^{n-2} + \ldots a_1 b^1 + a_0 b_0 \qquad 7.11$$

This series applies to both the decimal and the binary systems. In the decimal system $b = 10$ and a has values between 0 and 9 inclusive. Hence the decimal system of numbers can be built up as shown in the table of Fig. 7.13(a). In the binary system $b = 2$ and $a = 1$ or 0. The manner in which the binary system is built up is shown in Fig. 7.13(b).

FIG. 7.13(a). Decimal system of numbers

Thousands 10^3	Hundreds 10^2	Tens 10^1	Units 10^0
$0 \times 10^3 = 0$ $1 \times 10^3 = 1000$ $2 \times 10^3 = 2000$ $3 \times 10^3 = 3000$ etc.	$0 \times 10^2 = 0$ $1 \times 10^2 = 100$ $2 \times 10^2 = 200$ $3 \times 10^2 = 300$	$0 \times 10^1 = 0$ $1 \times 10^1 = 10$ $2 \times 10^1 = 20$ $3 \times 10^1 = 30$	$0 \times 10^0 = 0$ $1 \times 10^0 = 1$ $2 \times 10^0 = 2$ $3 \times 10^0 = 3$

FIG. 7.13(b). Binary system of numbers

Thousands 2^3	Hundreds 2^2	Tens 2^1	Units 2^0
$0 \times 2^3 = 0$ $1 \times 2^3 = 8$	$0 \times 2^2 = 0$ $1 \times 2^2 = 4$	$0 \times 2^1 = 0$ $1 \times 2^1 = 2$	$0 \times 2^0 = 0$ $1 \times 2^0 = 1$

The two systems are compared in the table of Fig. 7.14. The above tables indicate that the decimal scale is a scale of ten, while the binary system is a scale of two.

The binary system is of particular value for the operation of digital computers since the valves or transistors used to represent the integers are essentially two state devices being either 'on' or 'off', corresponding to conduction and absence of conduction respectively. Hence 'off' can conveniently represent a 'zero', while 'on' can be used to represent a 'one'.

In some cases, as will be seen below, the output of an analogue-to-digital converter may be simply a set of pulses, the total number of which is proportional to the analogue quantity. In such cases the first operation performed in the digital machine will be the conversion from digital data in serial form to the corresponding binary form.

With certain other analogue-to-digital converters the possibility of ambiguous output arises, particularly with the reading types

FIG. 7.14. Comparison of decimal binary, and cyclic binary systems

Decimal	Binary Code	Cyclic Binary Code
0	0	0
1	1	1
2	10	11
3	11	10
4	100	110
5	101	111
6	110	101
7	111	100
8	1000	1100
9	1001	1101
10	1010	1111
11	1011	1110
12	1100	1010
13	1101	1011
14	1110	1001
15	1111	1000
16	10000	11000
17	10001	11001
18	10010	11011
19	10011	11010
20	10100	11110
21	10101	11111
22	10110	11101
23	10111	11100
24	11000	10100
25	11001	10101
26	11010	10111
27	11011	10110
28	11100	10010
29	11101	10011
30	11110	10001
31	11111	10000
32	100000	110000
..	......	......

discussed in Section 3 below. In such cases the conversion of analogue signals to the corresponding digital quantity expressed in cyclic-permuted, or Gray code, (Refs. 7.13 and 7.14) reduces the possibility of ambiguity very considerably. The Gray code is given in the table of Fig. 7.14. It will be noticed that, unlike the ordinary binary code, only one digit changes in going from one value to the next. The significance of this property of the code will become apparent later. If cyclic-permuted binary code is used in this manner the first operation in the digital computer will be the conversion to ordinary binary code.

Analogue-to-digital converter devices take many forms. Nevertheless they may be divided for convenience into several main types. These are described in survey articles by Burke (Ref. 7.15) and Lippel (Ref. 7.16). A further article by Lippel (Ref. 7.17) is useful in that it discusses the use of digital techniques in measuring systems, and takes an automatic machine tool as an example. Accuracy and 'granularity' in mixed analogue and digital systems are considered and various other converter devices discussed. Some of the main types of analogue-to-digital converters are given below. Their variety is greater than that of the digital-to-analogue converters considered in a later section.

7.5.1 *Analogue-to-digital converters*

Type 1. *Direct counting converters.* Under this heading are considered devices in which the output comprises a train of unit pulses, the total number of which is proportional to the analogue quantity. An example of this type of converter might be a time interval encoder in which an oscillator output is gated to yield a train of pulses such that the number is proportional to the time interval. The number of pulses could then be counted using an electronic counter, so arranged that the output of the counter appears in appropriate form. The logical circuits which perform this operation are well established and are discussed in any standard text on digital computing.

Type 2. *Weighing converters.* In devices of this type a set of standard reference voltages are available against which the analogue quantity is compared or weighed. In some cases the converter is effectively a bridge in which the arms are automatically balanced until a null is reached. One type of digital voltmeter takes this form.

The digital voltmeter is a voltmeter with a high input impedance typically 10–100 MΩ. It forms a convenient, though expensive, output device for an analogue computer in that it presents the magnitude of an analogue voltage as a digital quantity with considerable precision. Typical resolution is ±0·01 volt over the range ±100 volts. Readings are displayed in the form of illuminated decimal digits complete with polarity sign and decimal point. Depending on type a measurement is completed and reading displayed at intervals of the order of one second. In more elaborate versions of the instrument, facilities are available for automatic recording of readings. Since the voltmeter is essentially a high-precision analogue-to-digital converter it may be used as the link between an analogue and a digital machine.

Type 3. *Reading type converters.* With devices in this category the magnitude of the analogue quantity is measured using optical, electromechanical, electronic or other means. The development of optical reading devices illustrates some of the general techniques employed to overcome the problems of this type of converter. For this reason optical devices are discussed in some detail.

Such devices include those which indicate angular position or linear displacement in binary fashion. They find applications in such fields as the automatic control of machine tools in addition to their use in analogue computing.

A schematic diagram of an angular position converter is shown in Fig. 7.15. A disc is mounted on the shaft for which the angular position is required. The disc is opaque except for certain segments of a set of concentric tracks on its face. These segments are transparent. A light source, arranged radially, illuminates each of the concentric tracks while a set of photocells is placed, facing the light source, on the opposite side of the disc. One photocell is opposite each track. The pattern of transparent segments on the disc is such that a unique pulse pattern in binary code appears from the photocells for each position of the disc. Since all the pulses appear simultaneously the output is known as a parallel output.

Angular position converters working on the above and similar principles have been used quite widely. A variety are available commercially. A detailed account of the problems associated with a rather more elaborate converter is given in Ref. 7.18. Here a single spot of light from a flying-spot scanner is used to scan a disc radially. A lens system focuses the pulses of light transmitted through the transparent sections of the disc and presents them to a single photocell. The train of output pulses represents the shaft setting in binary

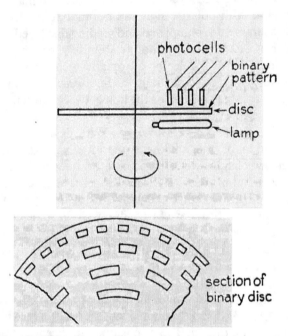

Fig. 7.15. Angular position analogue-to-digital converter

code. Since the pulses appear sequentially they represent a serial output.

Similar techniques may be employed to indicate linear displacement. In this case the pattern of transparent strips is arranged in linear fashion.

Either ordinary, or cyclic-permuted, binary code may be used for the patterns employed in the converters mentioned above. Figure 7.16

compares the patterns for the two cases. The advantage of the cyclic-permuted code over the straight binery code is illustrated for the decimal number 16. The effect of slight misalignment of, for example,

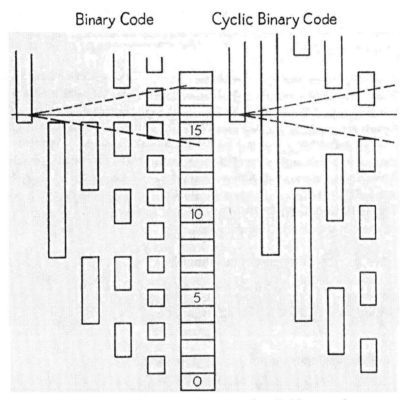

FIG. 7.16. Comparison of binary and cyclic binary codes

the reading heads is shown for both codes. For misalignment within the range indicated the binary output might take the values,

$$
\begin{aligned}
1\ 0\ 0\ 0\ 0 &= 16 \\
1\ 0\ 0\ 0\ 1 &= 17 \\
1\ 0\ 0\ 1\ 1 &= 19 \\
1\ 0\ 1\ 1\ 1 &= 23 \\
1\ 1\ 1\ 1\ 1 &= 31
\end{aligned}
$$

For the same range of misalignment when the cyclic code is employed the output is restricted to the values

$$1\ 1\ 0\ 0\ 0 = 16$$
$$1\ 1\ 0\ 0\ 1 = 17$$

Thus it is seen that the ambiguity is reduced to the least significant of the binary digits.

7.5.2 Digital-to-analogue converters

The elements of a simple digital-to-analogue converter are shown in the diagram of Fig. 7.17. A computing amplifier is used to sum the signals appearing at a set of input resistors. The input signals are the voltage pulses of a parallel output in binary code from a digital computer. Since each pulse in the set is of equal height, the ratios of the input resistors to the feedback resistor are arranged in such a manner that the input signals are multiplied by constants of 1, 2, 4, 8 and 16 corresponding to their position in the binary scale. For example at time t_1, the binary input is

$$1\ 0\ 1\ 0\ 1$$

The corresponding analogue output is

$$1 \times 16 + 0 \times 8 + 1 \times 4 + 0 \times 2 + 1 \times 1 = 21$$

A little later at time t_2, the binary input is

$$1\ 0\ 1\ 1\ 1$$

and the analogue output

$$1 \times 16 + 0 \times 8 + 1 \times 4 + 1 \times 2 + 1 \times 1 = 23$$

If the binary input signals are presented to the converter sufficiently rapidly the analogue output approximates to a smooth curve. The accuracy of the conversion depends in large measure on the precision with which the input pulses are generated.

Reference 7.19 is useful in that it gives details of other types of digital-to-analogue converters and also analogue-to-digital equipment. There is also a useful section on pen recorders and plotting tables.

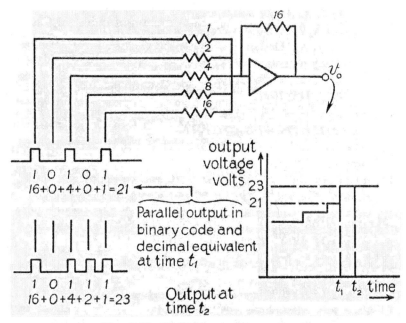

FIG. 7.17. Digital-to-analogue converter

REFERENCES

7.1. BAIRSTOW, L. *Applied Aerodynamics*, Longmans, London, 1939.

7.2. TRUXAL, J. *Automatic Feedback Control System Synthesis*, McGraw-Hill, New York, 1955.

7.3. CHANCE, B. *et al.* 'A quarter-square multiplier using a segmented parabolic characteristic', *Rev. sci. Instrum.*, **22**, 683, 1951.

7.4. CAMPBELL, L. L. *Galvanomagnetic and Thermomagnetic Effects*, Longmans, New York, 1923.

7.5. CHASMAR, R. P., and COHEN, E. 'An electrical multiplier utilizing the Hall effect in indium arsenide', *Electron. Engng*, **30**, 661, 1958.

7.6. MACNEE, A. B. 'An electronic differential analyser', *Proc. I.R.E.*, **37**, 1315, 1949.

7.7.   WASS, C. A. A. *An Introduction to Electronic Analogue Computers*, Ch. 7, Pergamon Press, London, 1956.

7.8.   KORN, G. A. 'Design and construction of universal function generating potentiometers', *Rev. sci. Instrum.*, **21**, 77, 1950.

7.9.   MYNALL, D. J. 'Electronic function generator', *Nature*, **159**, No. 4048, 743, 1947.

7.10. MACKAY, D. M. 'A high-speed electronic function generator', *Nature*, **159**, No. 4038, 406, 1947.

7.11. FIFER, S. *Analogue Computation*, Vol. II, Ch. 10, McGraw-Hill, New York, 1961.

7.12. HARTLEY, M. G. 'Versatile analogue computer for G.W. studies', *Control*, **4**, April p. 98 and May p. 103, 1961.

7.13. GRAY, H. J., LEVONIAN, P. V., and RUBINOFF, M. 'An analogue-to-digital converter for serial computing machines', *Proc. Inst. Radio Engrs.*, **41**, 1462, 1953.

7.14. HEATH, F. G. 'Pioneers of Binary Coding', *Journal I.E.E.*, **7**, 539, 1961.

7.15. BURKE, H. E. 'A survey of analogue-to-digital converters', *Proc. Inst. Radio Engrs*, **41**, 1455, 1953.

7.16. LIPPEL, B. 'A systematic survey of coders and decoders', *Inst. Radio Engrs National Convention Record, Part VIII*, 109, 1953.

7.17. LIPPEL, B. 'Interconversion of Analog and digital data in systems for measurement and control', *Proc. National Electronics Conf., Vol. VIII*, 636, 1952.

7.18. BARKER, R. H. 'A transducer for digital data-transmission systems', *Proc. I.E.E.*, **103B**, 42, 1956.

7.19. FIFER, S. *Analogue Computation*, Vol. II, Ch. 9, McGraw-Hill, New York, 1961.

Index

Date Due

PRINTED IN U. S. A.			CAT. NO. 23233